FROM LADYSMITH TO ARCHANGEL
The Language of War

VOLUME ONE

THE BOER WAR 1899-1902

best wishes James

By James Crowden

FLAGON
PRESS

From Ladysmith to Archangel
The Language of War
Volume One
The Boer War 1899-1902

Published by Flagon Press 2013
Forge House, Fore Street, Winsham, Chard,
Somerset TA20 4DY

© James Crowden 2013
www.james-crowden.co.uk

ISBN 978-0-9562778-5-5

British Library and Cataloguing-in-Production Data
A catalogue record for this book is available from
the British Library

Designed by Andrew Crane
Typeset in Cheltenham and News Gothic
Printed by Short Run Press Exeter

'Over the wire men or through it
Drive the charge home to the hill
Vain were our struggles and climbing
Deep stuck the barbs in our kilts.'

*Lines from a poem called 'The Battle of Magersfontein'
written by an anonymous soldier of the 2nd Black Watch.*

CONTENTS

PART 3 GETTING STUCK IN – BLACK WEEK

PART 4 BESIEGED

PART 5 GUERRILLA WAR

PART 6 **THE BITTER END**

PART 7 LONGUEVILLE DIARIES

PART 8 **THE LOST CAUSE**

Acknowledgements

I am very grateful to all those people who have helped me with research. To Justin Fleming for permission to use notes I had made about his grandfather, Trooper Theodore Fleming, Bethune's Mounted Infantry. To Liz Vernon for permission to use her mother's reminiscences about her father Private Harry Howlett of 18th Hussars. To Caroline Elkerton for the memories of Edith Monck-Mason's time as a nurse in South Africa. To Archie Hunter for permission to use a quote about boredom in The Siege of Ladysmith from his book *Kitchener's Sword-Arm – The life and campaigns of General Sir Archibald Hunter*. To Elisabeth Rowe for permission to quote from the letters of her great uncles: Lt Max Chevenix Trench and Lt Christopher Chevenix Trench. My thanks also go to Richard McKenzie, archivist at The Black Watch Castle and Museum in Perth for help with the Magersfontein poem and the debate about barbed wire. To my acupuncturist Rosemary Norton whose grandfather and great uncle, Reginald and Edward Longueville both served in the Coldstream Guards at the Battles of Belmont, Graspan, Modder River and Magersfontein. To Anthony and Christina Norton for the loan of Reginald Longueville's excellent diaries and permission to quote from them as well as using some of his historic photographs.

To Robert Boyle of Bisbrooke Hall for permission to use the photograph of his great grandfather Lt. Percy Evans-Freke of the Leicestershire Imperial Yeomanry. To James Payne of 'Through Their Eyes' for permission to use photographs from an album belonging to Captain Edward Simpson of the South African Light Horse.

I would also like to thank my partner Carla Sheills for her patience and dedicated support as we discussed the Boer War, often over breakfast, and for translating some Dutch and Afrikaans documents and letters. Also to her mother, Saar Steenkamp for her grandmother's memories of the Boer War internment camps. To Ignatius Steenkamp, Diane Kriegler-Massyn and Jan Human for helping to identify Tulip Grass. I am very grateful to Richard Watkins for proof reading and to Jan Moodie for casting his eye over the book before it went to print.

My thanks once again go to Andrew Crane, the artist and graphic designer who has stepped into the breach once more and designed the book with a very careful and thoughtful eye. And lastly to Short Run Press of Exeter for printing the book.

Nitpicking

South African Light Horse – taking tea with one the scouts

Introduction

This book is the first of a two volume work which takes the reader from South Africa to Northern Russia. It is primarily concerned with the language of war and the way that language was used to report on the war. The first volume is a short, fragmented history of the Boer War and includes previously unpublished accounts from both sides, as well as reports and newspaper articles that have not seen the light of day for over a hundred years.

The second volume wades through the awful quagmire of the First World War and ends up in Archangel. The work covers the years from 1899 to 1919, twenty very significant years and is comprised of poetry, anecdotes and vignettes, as well as some pithy notes on military history.

It is the underlying voices and speech patterns that fascinate me. Many of these excerpts are deliberately arranged as if they were poetry to emphasise the quality of language and to give a real voice to the person whose words they were. Some indeed are actual poems. I want to give a feeling of what it was like to be there, and how the war was received back home, either through letters or newspaper articles or diary excerpts. Some are direct verbatim accounts from interviews. Also many more stories are now emerging from the Boer side, and these are very important to balance up the vast weight of literature in English. Never before had there been so many war correspondents and never before had photography played such an important role in covering a war.

Language evolves, like warfare, and during the Boer War the British Army suddenly had to fight a modern war with modern weapons against a daring and elusive enemy who were, after all, mostly farmers. True the Boers had very good eyesight and modern rifles but the British Army had enormous reserves of manpower, heavy duty fire power and artillery, as well as a vast Empire to draw upon. Even so Britain very nearly lost the war and in the opening stages catastrophe followed catastrophe.

Some of the British victories were pyrrhic victories with great loss of life. It fast became a guerrilla war with new tactics and new rules, or at times no rules at all. The world watched and waited. The Kaiser rubbed his hands. And as the casualties began to mount, many people back home began to wonder what had caused the war in the first place, and why so many soldiers were dying of disease.

When the Boer War was over it still left many matters unresolved and slowly but surely the powers in Europe, lurched towards a much greater confrontation. Many of the army officers who were prominent in the First World War had cut their teeth in South Africa. They had also learnt more about defensive warfare, about trenches and barbed wire. A certain Major Douglas Haig and Major-General John French only just escaped from Ladysmith in a train under heavy fire. One well known young cavalry officer seeking the limelight, called Winston Churchill, was captured in an armoured train which had been ambushed near Chieveley. The man who later commanded the British troops at Gallipoli, General Sir Ian Hamilton, had been bottled up in the Siege of Ladysmith as had Colonel Henry Rawlinson, who eventually oversaw the evacuation of British troops from Archangel in September 1919.

But there were other fascinating links. Vincent Van Gogh's youngest brother Cornelis, who had worked on the railways, ended up fighting on the Boer side in a Dutch Commando. He was wounded, captured and died in a British army hospital. Some reports say he committed suicide. On the British side working as a stretcher bearer was a feisty Indian born lawyer called M. K. Gandhi. A rare collection of eccentric characters which included Lady Sarah Wilson, Winston's young and very attractive aunt, who became the first woman war correspondent reporting from inside the Siege of Mafeking for The *Daily Mail*.

To fully understand the origins of the First World War one has to first understand the Boer War and its effect on modern warfare. And rather like the Spanish Civil War it was a proxy war. It also had a wild and rich seam of stories which at the time captured the public imagination, but there was also a darker side which was kept from the public, and this has to be explored and acknowledged.

This research provided a fascinating insight into another world, where the 19th century and the 20th century briefly overlapped. Unearthing new sources and previously unpublished photographs was particularly enjoyable. It has also been the unravelling of a story about a war which should never have happened, and within that story the 'Language of War' became embedded in the narrative; a language that changed as the war progressed.

The book was written at high speed in three months flat and at times it felt more like scripting a radio programme on the hoof - there was such a rich diversity of voices. But if this small book intrigues people and encourages them to find out more about the Boer War then it will have done its job.

James Crowden October 2013

Part 1

Origins of the Boer War

Background

For many people today the Boer War is a faded, distant memory, lodged on the horizon – like an old photograph on the mantelpiece. It was the last in a long line of hard fought Victorian colonial wars in places like Afghanistan, Egypt, Sudan, Burma and lesser scraps on the North-West Frontier like Umbeyla, Malakand and Tirah. But it was very different to all of those wars, not just in scale but in tactics, ethics and weapons. The story as it unfolded gripped the world and changed forever the way that war was reported and indeed fought.

In some senses the Boer War was a civil war between the English and Afrikaans speaking inhabitants of South Africa. The word 'Boer' simply means farmer, so it should really be called 'The Farmer War'. To confuse matters still further, many English speakers fought on the Boer side and vice versa. There were also many international commandos. And caught between these two opposing forces was not only the civilian population, white, black and coloured but the vast army of local labourers, militia, guards and scouts, without whom neither side could function or even feed itself.

It was almost a war of language, and yet into this heady mix entered the economic impetus of diamond mining at Kimberley and the recent discovery of gold on the Witwatersrand, which provided irresistible bait for people like Cecil Rhodes and Alfred Beit who were not above influencing foreign policy for their own financial and political gain. The love of gold and diamonds coupled with a full measure of Imperial pride was therefore stacked against a handful of bible reading farmers who wanted simply to get on with their lives farming in a quiet backwater. They had after all carved out their own Republics of Transvaal and Orange Free State. It was on the face of it a very unfair match.

The British Army was very unprepared for such a war. Their 'enemy' in this war were not wily tribesmen or religious fanatics but often highly intelligent well read farmers and lawyers who evolved daring new guerrilla tactics to deal with the British Army and its Imperial fighting machine. Most of the Boers' weapons were very modern and came from either Germany or France. They also often spoke English as well as Afrikaans and many were either of Dutch or of French Huguenot extraction, so in a sense it was a European war, fought on African soil. For the Boers it was called the Anglo-Boer War, and in Afrikaans the 'War of Liberation' or the 'English War'.

There were also foreign commandos just as there were International Brigades in the Spanish Civil War. Indeed the Boer War is in some ways to the First War what the Spanish Civil War was to the Second War. A proxy war where new tactics and weapons could be tried out. There were also many foreign war correspondents. There were cameras, telegraph systems, cables, even film footage. Newspapers devoured the reports of how the fighting was going, and many even at home in Britain secretly admired the under dog. There was, at least at the beginning of the war, a great sense of fair play, on both sides, and it was often called the 'Last of the Gentleman's Wars' where they did not fight on Sundays. They often called truces to deal with the wounded and exchanged medical supplies. It was also a very public war where propaganda and censorship played an important role in swaying public opinion.

But as the guerrilla war dragged on it became more and more ruthless, and was anything but gentlemanly. Thousands of farms were burnt and the women and children were systematically herded into refugee camps which were now called 'concentration camps'. A term which had evolved during fighting in Cuba and the Philippines when both the Spanish and the American army used them as internment camps: the original phrase being *reconcentrados* (reconcentration camps). Forcibly removing civilians from their land for military reasons was nothing new as many reservations for Native American Indians were set up in this way.

The term 'concentration camp' has now become so overloaded with darker meanings from Second World War and the Holocaust that some Afrikaner academics such as André Wessels advise that the term 'internment camps' is more accurate and preferable.

So the British were not entirely alone in using camps as a means to an end, but it was the unprecedented scale of them which caused alarm as well as many unnecessary deaths from malnutrition and disease. It was Queen Victoria's last war. She died in January 1901, over a year before it ended.

The First Boer War

To understand the Second Boer War (1899-1902) which lasted over two and half years one has to understand the events of the First Boer War (1880-1881) which only lasted about three months. This earlier, but decisive war, is largely forgotten today, at least in Britain, because it was nothing more than a string of small but humiliating defeats for the British army. After the end of the Zulu

Wars, which included the well known battles of Isandlwana, Rorke's Drift and Ulundi, the British vainly thought they could get their hands on the Transvaal with its rich diamond and gold mines. Greed reinforced with the Martini-Henry rifle.

The Boers, who had trekked from Cape Colony to Transvaal in the 1830s and 1840s, however had other ideas. Transvaal formally declared independence from Cape Colony on 16 December 1880 and laid siege to various British army camps. They promptly ambushed a British convoy at Bronkhorstspruit and in a battle lasting just fifteen minutes, 156 British soldiers were killed or wounded. The rest were taken prisoner. This was

In memory of 24 NCOs & Men of 3rd Battalion 60th Royal Rifles who fell in action 8 Feb 1881 at the Battle of Ingogo

followed by further British defeats at Laing's Nek, Ingogo and Majuba Hill in Northern Natal.

In this last action in February 1881 about 400 farmers attacked a similar size force of British soldiers who had foolishly camped up on top of Majuba Hill without even digging in. Next morning they were caught napping and were eventually driven off the top by the Boers, who had to work their way round and fight up the hill, which in places was very steep. This resulted in heavy casualties for the British: ninety-two dead, 134 wounded, and fifty-nine captured. Even Major General Colley was killed. It was a bit Gilbert and Sullivan. Boer casualties for Majuba were one killed and five wounded.

Boers in action 1881

Interestingly the famous comic song from the *Pirates of Penzance* – 'I am the Very Model of a Modern Major-General' was aired only two years earlier on the stage in London in 1879. Lines which must have haunted the British establishment. They were in fact modelled not on Major-General Colley but on General Garnet Wolseley who had tried to modernise the army. In early versions of the libretto, 'Mauser rifle' is 'Chassepot rifle' a forerunner of the Mauser, which had a rotating bolt system. Later, the Mauser became the more widely used rifle and the more familiar to audiences, so the lyric was changed.

Major-General Sir George Pomeroy Colley was however no sluggard. He had been to staff college at Sandhurst and had come out top of his class with distinction. He was a very well educated man, always got up two hours before breakfast and taught himself Russian, chemistry and political economy. He was also an accomplished artist in water-colours, and spent much of his leave on sketching tours, not only on Dartmoor, but in Normandy and Spain. He certainly did not lead from the rear and had also fought in China and Ashanti. British fire power was fine against spears and clubs. But the Boer farm boys were very different adversaries and did not play by the book. They were all excellent riflemen and had to fend for themselves from an early age. Their women were often good shots and could also ride well.

The Boer Commandant General was Piet Joubert, of French Huguenot stock, who later helped re-arm the Transvaal. So the motley crew of Boer farm boys had not only taught the British army a salutary lesson in field craft, camouflage, guerrilla tactics, ambush, fire and movement and above all marksmanship, but they had put the British Empire into crisis mode.

After peace negotiations had been agreed, which recognised the Boer right to self determination, things temporarily settled down.

A Vein of Remarkable Richness

Three years later on 8 September 1884, gold was found in the Witwatersrand by an impoverished geologist with the wonderful name of Frederick Pine Theophilus Struben. Witwatersrand which means 'white water's ridge' is just outside Johannesburg. It was a key moment in the history of the Transvaal and life for the Afrikaners was never quite the same afterwards. The moment that Fred Struben actually discovered gold is described in his own words by William Macdonald who interviewed him in the 1920s and is recorded in his book called *The Romance of the Golden Rand*.

'Leaving camp soon after breakfast
I was fossicking about for several hours
Without finding anything of value.

The sun was pouring down from a cloudless sky.
And I was tired of walking over rough and rocky ground
And carrying various samples I had collected on the way…

I determined however to keep moving and at midday
I was down in the valley that runs at the bottom of the range.
Suddenly I looked up at the southern range

and saw that a disturbance had taken place in the rocks.
I immediately conceived the idea
of the possibility of a reef in that formation.

The thought gave me new life and vigour.
All depression and tiredness left me
and I moved quickly forward to the spot.

I was not wrong in my opinion
for there I found a reef cutting right
through the displaced strata.

Hastily I broke up a piece of the surface rock
and took it to a stream nearby.
I crushed the stone on large flat rock…and panned it.

Imagine my joy when out of a little bit of rock,
there came almost a teaspoon full of gold,
the pan being literally covered with it.

I was so astonished with the quantity of metal
that I was still doubtful if it really was gold.
I set off at once to my camp and tested it.

It was then that I realised that I had found
a vein of remarkable richness
and great value.

I stood at my tent door alone.
There was no one to speak to
in the vast solitude of the veld.'

Frederick and his brother Harry Struben then got to work
with staking a claim and extracting the gold. The vein
that they had tapped into called the Confidence Reef,
eventually ran out but not before thousands of others had
poured into the Transvaal and this led to the famous gold
rush of 1886. Harry Struben also helped Paul Kruger, the
President of the Transvaal to work out a series of laws
regulating gold prospecting and mining.

The discovery was monumental and as Fred Struben continues:

'Years of suffering, ridicule and disappointment
came before me in a flash. I remembered
that the only thing left to me through it all

was that strange unconquerable confidence
within me that one day I would strike a rich gold field.
Then as I looked over the barren veld and desolate kopjes

I saw a vision of a gold bearing formation
that would bring millions of capital into South Africa
and provide work for thousands of miners.'

The Confidence Reef was on the farm at Wilgespruit eleven miles from Johannesburg on the West Rand and two and a half miles north-west of Roodepoort.

The Jameson Raid

The Jameson Raid which came from Rhodesia and Matabeleland in the north was planned by none other than Cecil Rhodes himself, but carried out by Leander Starr Jameson, otherwise known as 'Dr Jim' or 'Lanner'. It was a botched and crude attempt to overthrow Paul Kruger in a stage managed coup and it failed miserably.

The force of 600 horsemen included 400 men from the Matabeleland Mounted Police as well as many volunteers. The force was equipped with rifles, a few Maxim machine guns and about half a dozen light artillery pieces. Just what you need for a picnic in the Transvaal. Dr Jameson led the force and the intention was to link up with an *Uitlander* uprising in Johannesburg, an uprising which never materialised.

The raid ended up as yet another humiliating defeat. They rode for a day or two, cut the wires to Cape Town but not to Pretoria. Some say they cut the barbed wire fence by mistake when under the influence of... certain alcoholic substances.

So the Boers and everyone else knew what was going on. There were skirmishes at Krugersdorp and Doornkop, about twenty miles from Johannesburg. The force was eventually surrounded and outgunned. They lost about sixty-five men in all. Only one Boer was killed.

Dr Jameson was forced to surrender to Piet Cronjé and was imprisoned. Later he was handed over to the British who took him home to London where he was tried and sentenced to fifteen months in Holloway. A mere slap on the wrist. He became a national hero. The British South Africa Company was forced to pay the Transvaal government almost £1 million in compensation. Some members of the Johannesburg Reform Committee including Cecil Rhodes's brother were imprisoned and then put on trial for High Treason. Some were even sentenced to be hung, others were given fifteen year sentences. Most in the end got off with stiff fines. Some

say they were covering up for Joseph Chamberlain and other politicians who had sanctioned the raid. Even today it is something of a mystery.

Interestingly Rudyard Kipling wrote his famous poem 'If' as a tribute to Jameson. 'If you can keep your head when all about you are losing theirs' etc, etc which makes the poem even

Leander Star Jameson

more revealing. It was written in 1895 but not published till 1910. In August 1914 *The Times* published the poem on the announcement of the outbreak of the First World War.

Even more significant, however, was the 'Kruger' telegram from the Kaiser Wilhelm II sent to Paul Kruger, President of the Transvaal Republic, only twenty-four hours after Dr Jameson's capture.

> *'I express to you my sincere congratulations that you and your people, without appealing to the help of friendly powers, have succeeded, by your own energetic action against the armed bands which invaded your country as disturbers of the peace, in restoring peace and in maintaining the independence of the country against attack from without.'*

The Kaiser, in effect, not only officially recognised the Boer Republic and put them on an international footing, but he congratulated the Boers on their bravery and competence and was seen to promise them help in the

Jameson and his chums make their last stand at Doornkop.
2 January 1896 Painting by Richard Caton Woodville

Cecil Rhodes

Paul Kruger

future, if they were ever threatened again by the British. The contents of the Kruger telegram were leaked to the press and there were anti-German riots. German sailors were even attacked in London.

Trying to pour oil over troubled waters the Kaiser sent a conciliatory letter to his grand-mother, none other than Queen Victoria herself, insisting that:

'Never was the Telegram intended as a step against England or your Government.'

In the meantime the Kaiser enjoyed sailing his new 128 ft yacht *Meteor II* at the Royal London Yacht Club. In June 1896 his yacht built in Glasgow and crewed by men from Gosport and Portsmouth passed the finishing line at Gravesend thirteen minutes ahead of the Prince of Wales's *Britannia*. The crowds were silent. *Meteor II* also won the Nore-to-Dover race a few days later, beating *Britannia* this time by nine minutes five seconds. Interestingly the much anticipated race at Cowes that year never happened as both yachts were involved in a collision with two other yachts a few days before. The Kaiser was very keen on racing at Cowes and had won in 1893 with *Meteor I*. Osborne House was not far away and he wanted to win again right under Queen Victoria's nose. The Kaiser was also jealous of Granny's navy and not long afterwards he instigated a massive ship building programme all of his own. Only this time the ships had real guns not sails and were kitted out with radios and armour plate.

To the Boers, the Jameson raid was seen as a 'Declaration of War', and in its aftermath the Boers came to Europe to buy weapons. In effect they were arming themselves ready for the Second Boer War and it was the gold which was paying for their weapons. Germany, France and Austria were all to ready to do business. The greed and intentions of certain individuals linked with an aggressive foreign policy had in effect put the stability of the whole of South Africa at risk. The arms race was on and South Africa was as good a place as any for a proxy war against the British Empire. They were all sailing very close to the wind. They just needed an excuse to start. And in the wings journalists and war correspondents were waiting in their droves with pocket note books and pencils at the ready.

Balloons were filled with hydrogen

Ostrich feathers were very popular

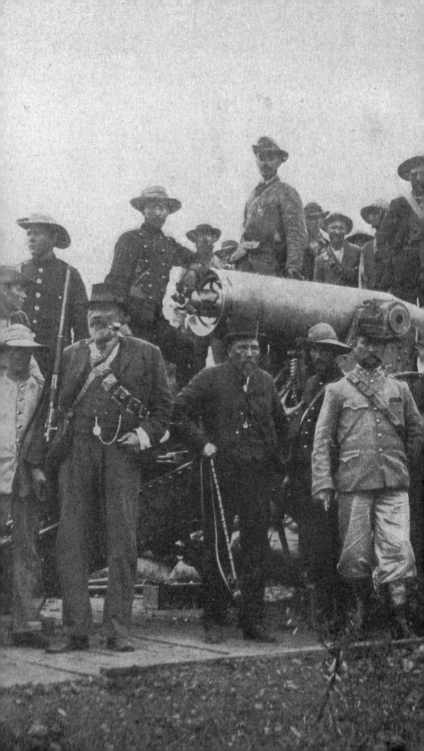

Part 2

Sliding Into War

The Language of War

We use the word Commando
As if it was our own
Like anorak and kayak and bivouac slipped in
Under cover of darkness by the back door.

Like guerrilla, hooker, zariba and sangar,
Dekko, shufti and Aide-de-Camp.
'Time spent in reconnaissance is seldom wasted'
In the bundu, if you get my drift –

Mine's a pint of laager when on trek.
Like 'Hit and Run' and 'Scorched Earth'
Language has its own twists and turns
Cul-de-sacs out of which there is no sense of return

A fait accompli you might say.
Mafeking Night and Scouting for Boys,
The double entendre, not forgetting of course
That it was the Boer commandos

Who brought the British Army to its knees.
Perhaps the Kaiser was a little unwise
To send a congratulatory telegram
So soon after the Jameson Raid.

Young Boer Bucks displaying captured British Army Lee-Metford rifles with distinctive magazines and long range sights. The other men at the back have Mausers.

Slim Piet

Piet Joubert was a clever chap
A clever chap was he,
So he ordered lots of rifles
To even up the odds.

Majuba and Jameson,
He never drank the stuff,
But he liked the way the farm boys
Had kicked the British butt.

Six and thirty thousand
He ordered to be precise
Old Martini-Henrys
Fine for the Zulu Wars

Fine at four hundred yards
Stopped dead men in their tracks
Twelve rounds a minute –
Kicked like a mule.

But the new breed of farm boys
Wanted something lighter
A little bit more modern
A little bit more sleek.

And with the next war brewing up,
They'd need the latest gear,
To tickle the British army
In its perky derriere.

So Kruger gave him gold
To fill his pockets large
And right away he strolled
Into Europe's rich bazaars.

'Look here my man get real.
It's a Mauser you must buy
Five rounds per magazine,
Sixty – the bandolier.'

Even the powder's smokeless,
They can't see where you lie.
The latest little trick
To help even more men die.

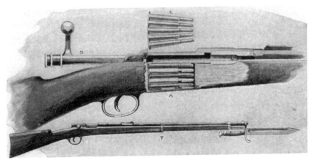

Mauser
The Boers, unlike the British, never used bayonets

There's Mauser '93 and Mauser '95
I am sure the Kaiser will approve
This little export deal. Ten or is it twenty?
Million rounds you are after?

That should do for starters.
Then maybe you will visit Herr Krupp?
And see what he's got on offer
A little howitzer or two wouldn't go amiss.

There's the French *Soixante-Quinze*
A dainty little field gun, quick firing
Q.F. to be precise and the new
Creusot. Only twice the size.

Le Creusot 'Long Tom' 155 mm at the siege of Mafeking.
Note the men wearing Staats Artillerie uniforms

37 mm Automatic Machine Gun 'Pom-Pom'

Ah Yes the Maxim Nordenfelt?
I was forgetting... I'll take
A few of those as well... I think
That's all on Kruger's little shopping list.

Piet Joubert was a clever chap
A clever chap was he
So he ordered lots of rifles
To even up the odds.

Last Chance Saloon

I

They chose a room close to the railway station
Avenues lined with jacaranda trees –
Adelstrop on the edge of the highveld.

No one got off – And no one really got on.
Long table – long talks,
In truth they were up against the buffers.

President Steyn broke the ice – introduced Kruger
Joked with Sir Alfred,
'You may have seen his name in the newspapers?'

M.T. Steyn, Lord Milner, F.W.Reitz and Paul Kruger
Bloemfontein Conference 31 May - 5 June 1899

Kruger even poked the High Commissioner in the ribs,
Half in jest – played the fool
But deep down both knew it was no joke.

An odd pair: Kruger, in Voortrekker saddle,
Bible and biltong his only tutors.
Shot his first lion at fourteen, wore black suit,

Top hat and gloves, as if going to a funeral.
Stolid, stubborn, wily and patriachal –
He at least had tasted war – knew its bitter consequences.

Sir Alfred, on the other hand, dapper Balliol man,
Lawyer and classical scholar
Almost thirty years his junior – Civil Administrator

High Commissioner – Governor of the Cape
Made polite but increasingly impossible
Demands that irked the Boer leaders no end.

II

All matters except the Independence
Of the Republics were on the table
And under discussion. 'All, All All.'

Franchise, Uitlanders and the English Language
Each delicate issue laid out
On the table like a Royal Flush.

Even taxation and the vagaries
Of the dynamite monopoly were discussed
Along with compensation for the Jameson Raid.

Kruger, slowly puffed his pipe – stood his ground
In a cloud of tobacco smoke –
Then on the third day offered what he could

His own prepared Reform Bill –
Came at least half way or more.
But that was not enough for Sir Alfred

And as Jan Smuts, Cambridge double-first
Attorney – Middle Temple
And admirer of Walt Whitman noted down –

'Sir Alfred – as sweet as honey but there is something
in his intelligent eyes which tells me
that he is very dangerous, more dangerous than Rhodes.'

Sir Alfred deliberately stalled – gave no ground
Yet the gap that they had to bridge was so small –
A scaffold plank would have done the trick.

III

By Monday Sir Alfred suddenly broke off the talks,
Without even waiting to hear
from his boss back in London:

Jan Smuts and his faithful Mauser

The Secretary of State for the Colonies,
The father of Neville, no less,
'Peace in Our Time', Joe Chamberlain.

So close at times, yet none could quite trust
The other. The last chance thrown away
For want of pen and paper – a signature or two.

Even a squiggle would have done the trick.
But Sir Alfred had a new mistress
Waiting for him discreetly back in Cape Town.

'It is our country that you want'
Kruger finally said with tears welling up in his eyes.
They were so very close – only a whisper away

Yet there was a strange kind of silence
In the room – as if they both knew deep down
That thousands of lives now hung in the balance.

And if you listened very carefully
You could hear the Afrikaner clock ticking –
And in the distance the clink of cavalry spurs.

Bloemfontein
31 May – 5 June 1899

Sir Alfred Milner deep in thought

*Exactly a year after the end of the Bloemfontein conference,
British troops finally entered Pretoria – 5 June 1900.
Many thought it was the end of the war. It wasn't.*

*Heavy artillery was very useful at the beginning of the war
but of limited use during the long guerrilla campaign.*

Ultimatum

For months they stood there shuffling their feet
Backwards and forwards
Buying time while Smuts helped Kruger

Write the Ultimatum which dragged both sides into the abyss.
Stockpiling ammunition – checking weapons
Zeroing in their sights on each other.

'Gold will cause our land to be soaked in blood'
Even Slim Piet reluctantly wondered if it was
All really necessary. This would be a very different war.

Trust in 'God and the Mauser'
'Queen and Bayonet'
'Pull old Kroojers Whiskers', 'Remember Majuba'.

The young bloods had their young blood up
Thirsty for another go,
But the Boers already had them by the short and curlies.

The Ultimatum came and went:
Forty-eight hours to remove all troops
From the borders and high seas. Expired 5 o'clock local time.

Ferreira, Jumper, Bonanza and Robinson Deep
All went silent.
Miners wisely scarpered, legged it down to Natal.

9 October 1899

Reply of Great Britain

Her Majesty's Government
have received with great regret
the peremptory demands
of the Government of the South African Republic
conveyed in your telegram of 9 October, No. 3.

You will inform
the Government of the South African Republic,
in reply, that the conditions demanded by
the Government of the South African Republic
are such as Her Majesty's Government
deem it impossible to discuss.

10 October 1899

Ammunition train and soldiers at Modder River

Sharks – The Passage Out

'Jumped on a cattle boat – Tilbury
God what an eye opener that was
Signed on the dotted line. Worked my passage

Eighteen shillings a month. Absolute hell
You know what it's like in a storm
And those poor buggers shovelling coal down below.

Wouldn't have had their job for all the tea in China.
Tended the horses, they hated the tropics
Threw the carcasses overboard

Sharks always circling
Buggers never paid us a cent.
Cape Town full of wind jammers

Skelton crews stripped clean.
All gone up country. Joined the Colonials.
Bethune's Mounted Infantry. Irregulars.

Very Irregular indeed – One of the finest units
Out there – Swashbuckling
Load of bandits, wild bunch of cattle thieves.

Five shillings a day and slouch hats.
No wonder nobody wanted the Queen's shilling
Used to desert from the regulars like flies.'

Trooper Theodore Fleming, Bethune's Mounted Infantry

Capture of *Mosquito*

Towards sunset Vellum appeared with a note
from Sergeant Matthews. It ran as follows:
'The armoured train captured;
its fifteen occupants all killed.
Boers opened fire on the train with field artillery'.

It seemed to be impossible that men
were killing each other only a few short miles away.

The herd of cattle we had passed came into view,
and caught sight of the water in the dam.

It was curious to see the whole herd,
some five or six hundred beasts, break into a clumsy canter,
and, with a bellowing noise, dash helter-skelter to the water –
big oxen with huge branching horns,
meek-eyed cows, young bullocks, and tiny calves,
all joining in the rush for a welcome drink
after a long hot day on the veldt.

The last news that came in that evening
was that all the wires were cut north and south of Mafeking,
and the telegraphists fled, as their lives had been threatened.

Lady Sarah Wilson October 1899

Signalling

Dash Dot Dot Dot
Dash Dash Dash
Dot
Dot Dash Dot

Dot Dash Dash
Dot Dash
Dot Dash Dash

A parting gift from mother
Heliographs in the sun
Officers used to signal
To one another from kopje to kopje
With their watch cases in the sun

Col Rhodes heliographing his brother Cecil Rhodes in Kimberley

Engraved and round,
Dear Mum. Hit the spot
Not many of them survived.
Snipers… Second hand
Second Lieutenants.
The trigger finger itchy.

They soon got the message.
A parting gift from the Boers.

All in the timing.
Must Dash Dot.

**Trooper Theodore Fleming
Bethune's Mounted Infantry**

*Colonel Kekewich and his Staff waiting to welcome
General French outside Kimberley 15 February 1900*

Hedgehog

Yesterday Thacknell of the 18th Hussars
Better known as Hedgehog,
Was out towards Landsman's Drift
Buffalo River with six men.

He saw a police station some distance ahead
In possession of the Boers,
The two policemen and their horses
Being taken prisoner or killed.

He got up to within 600 yards to have a look
And thirty of them bolted away.
He and six men followed them
And when the Boers saw such a small party

They turned, broke up into small parties
And tried to surround them.
Thacknell wisely made tracks like smoke
And went back by a different road…

**Lt Max Chevenix Trench
69th Field Battery Royal Artillery.
Dundee, Sunday 15 October 1899**

Spies

Leicesters caught two spies this morning
Making a sketch map of the camp

From a place about a mile away
From the southward. They also found

Their horses, which were real beauties
In a donga a few hundred yards away…

Both men were officers of the Staats Artillerie.
In the afternoon Tyler Goff and I rode out

To a high ridge under Impale to see
If we could see any of them about.

We saw their camp smoke
About 6 p.m. some six miles away.

The Boers are now closing round
From three directions.

Lt Max Chevenix Trench
Dundee, Wednesday, 18 October 1899

Mark Twain on the Boer War

'I talk the war with both sides –
always waiting until the other man introduces the topic.
Then I say, "My head is with the British,
but my heart and such rags of morals as I have
are with the Boer –
now we will talk unembarrassed
and without prejudice."
And so we discuss and have no trouble.'

'A sordid & criminal war, & in everyway shameful & excuseless.'

'I think England sinned in getting into a war
in South Africa which she could have avoided
without loss of credit or dignity -
just as I think we have sinned in crowding ourselves
into a war in the Philippines on the same terms.'

'Mr. Churchill knows all about war and nothing about peace.
War might be very interesting to persons
who like that sort of entertainment,
but I have never enjoyed it myself.'

'God created war so that Americans would learn geography.'

Early morning Patrol

Coffee with the Boers

I now saw the interior of a typical
Dutch house, with the family at home.
The *vrou* came forward with hand
outstretched in the awkward Boer fashion.

The Dutch do not shake hands;
they simply extend a wooden member,
which you clasp, and the greeting is over.

I had to go through this performance
in perfect silence with about seven or eight children
of various ages, a grown-up daughter,
and eight or ten men, most of whom followed us
into the poky little room which appeared to serve
as a living-room for the whole family.

Although past ten o'clock, the remains of breakfast
were still on the table, and were not appetizing to look at.
We sat down on chairs placed in a circle,
the whole party commencing to chatter volubly,
and scarcely a word being intelligible to me.

Presently the *vrou* brought me a cup of coffee
in a cracked cup and saucer.
Not wishing to give offence, I tried to swallow it;
the coffee was not bad, if one could only
have dissociated it from that dreadful breakfast-table.

I then produced some cigarettes,
and offered them to the male element.

They were enchanted, laid aside their pipes,
and conversed with more animation than ever;
but it was only occasionally that I caught
a word I could understand;
the sentence *twee tozen Engelman dood*
recurred with distressing frequency
and enabled me to grasp that their conversation
was entirely about the war.

Lady Sarah Wilson December 1899

Drawing of Lady Sarah Wilson in South Africa during the Second
Boer War, published in The Black and White Budget Transvaal Special
No 8. Caption reads "A brave woman. Lady Sarah Wilson, who is
acting both as nurse and correspondent at Mafeking".
She was slightly wounded by a shell fragment.

Notes: Part 2
Sliding Into War

Language of War

Often small words slip into our language from foreign wars and stay there for generations. Commando is one in particular. The word stems from the Afrikaans word **kommando**. These were formed often on family lines or regional units. Their commanders were naturally enough called **kommandants**. They were reasonably democratic and elected their leaders and everyman was obliged to turn up to defend his area with a horse and rifle and enough rations for five or six days. So they could form mobile units of what we now called mounted infantry rather than cavalry units. The first 'Commando Law' was brought in by the Dutch East India Company in the Cape during the 1650s. First English usage 1834. However the singular word 'commando' to denote a member of that elite fighting unit only came into use in Britain during the Second World War.

Anorak although often worn by commandos did not appear in the English language till 1924 no doubt because of the Greenland expeditions. The word **kayak** was used at much the same time. Even the word 'expedition' was a military term used between the wars to denote a major undertaking either for exploration or mountaineering. **Bivouac** is derived from the French via Alsatian *biwacht* meaning double or night watch, commonly used in the British Army during the Napoleonic Wars.

Hooker is a term for a prostitute that came into vogue during the American Civil War, named after the band of girls that followed General Joseph Dalton Hooker and the army of the Potomac. The 'girls' were known as 'General Hooker's Army'. He had quite a reputation as a hard drinking ladies man and gave lavish parties for his girls. The term 'hooker' meaning a prostitute was in use in New York as early as 1845 and refers to streetwalkers at a certain Manhattan ferry point called Corlaer's Hook. During the Civil War there was a large red-light district in Washington known as 'Hooker's Division'. Hooker is not to be confused with the Galway hooker, which is a fine looking sailing vessel found on the west-coast of Ireland.

The term *guerrilla* means 'little war' in Spanish and was picked up by the British army during the Peninsular War in 1809, where many small bands of Spanish guerrilla fighters took on the French. The term *guerrilla* also applies to a particular type of warfare.

Zariba is a thorn enclosure which was used to defend a campsite or village and also to keep cattle and livestock in one place. Also used for defence in the Sudanese and Somali Wars where it came into British army terminology. *Sangar* is a small man-made wall or breast work usually in a half circle made of stones to provide cover and temporary fortification where the digging of trenches is not possible. It derives from the Urdu and Persian word *sang* which means stone. As a term it was widely used on the North-West Frontier and is still used in the army today. In Northern Ireland it was used to denote a sand-bagged sentry post on the perimeter of army bases.

Other Indian terms have also crept in and stayed. The same is true of *dekko* which means 'a quick look' from the Hindi *dekho,* and *shufti* comes from the Arabic meaning much the same thing. Many of the troops in the Boer War had also served in Egypt and the Sudan. Once the army gets hold of a useful word it rarely lets go and many of these phrases have crept into everyday speech.

Aide-de-Camp or A.D.C. was first used in 1670, though gained popularity during the Napoleonic and Crimean wars. A.D.C.s are a vital link in the chain of command carrying orders, often to keep the general on the straight and narrow with info, gen and gin and tonic.

Bundu means outback or wild region. **Drift** is Dutch or Afrikaans for a ford in a river. Hence Rorke's Drift. **Laager** is not a beer but a Boer encampment usually constructed with wagons, but can be more permanent: i.e. winter quarters. It is often still used by cavalry regiments in their tanks to denote a night camp. Not to be confused with a certain type of German beer much drunk by squaddies. There is however a common root. The term **lager** comes from **ligrs**, which is Gothic for 'a place of lying or lying down'. Something you would definitely have to do after eight pints or when you are **laagered** up.

Trek is yet another Afrikaans word that has come into our language, and originally denoted the long laborious journeys undertaken by ox wagons. It comes from the Dutch to travel or to pull. Today it usually means to travel on foot in mountainous areas. The term **Voortrekkers** means 'those who pull ahead' and was used to describe those families that made the Great Trek eastwards in the 1830s and 1840s from the Cape to what is now Transvaal, Orange Free State and Natal. **Trek** first appeared in English in about 1850.

Hit and Run raids and **Scorched Earth** are self explanatory – both accurate military terms. Scorched

Scorched earth

earth meant what it says. Farms were burnt, crops and grassland were burnt, animals were killed and left to rot. The Boer families evicted in a matter of minutes and were then carted off to camps. The aim was to deny food, rations and intelligence to the commandos still on the run. Psychologically it backfired and made the **bitter enders** fight even harder. The women and children were none too pleased either. Many of the British soldiers hated this work as it was not warfare as they knew it.

Mafeking Night was a vast celebration to commemorate the end of the Siege of Mafeking on 17 May 1900. To 'maffick' means to celebrate extravagantly. One old man in a pub in the Chilterns when I asked if he had ever been to London, said 'Yes... on Mafeking Night'. It was very unusual for the British to dance in the streets with joy. Indeed, to let their hair down at all. To maffick also means 'to celebrate with riotous rejoicings'. ie when things got out of hand.

Scouting for Boys is a reference to the man in charge of the Siege of Mafeking – Colonel Robert Baden-Powell who after the war set up The Scout Movement which is now worldwide. His skills were learnt mainly from Zulu scouts and trackers in the 1880s and he put them to very good use during the Boer War. The first Scout camp was held on Brownsea Island in Dorset in 1907. **Scouting for Boys – A Handbook for Instruction in Good Citizenship** was his first guide to good scouting. It has sold over 100 million copies worldwide.

Cover of first part of Scouting for Boys, January 1908

References to the Kaiser and the Jameson Raid are covered in the Introduction. The Language of War can be taken on many different levels and like warfare itself is always evolving.

Slim Piet

Petrus Jacobus Joubert (1834-1900) better known as Piet Joubert was a farmer and a lawyer of French Huguenot extraction whose family originally came from Provence. He became Commandant General of the Boer army at the age of 34 and had been their general at Majuba Hill and was responsible for the tactics which gave the British army a bloody nose. Piet Joubert was anything but slim. The nickname 'Slim Piet' actually means 'Clever Pete'.

Piet Joubert

After the Jameson Raid in 1896 the Boers realised that they had to rearm. Piet Joubert ordered 36,000 Martini-Henry rifles which were black powder single shot heavy duty rifles with a hefty .45 lead slug. Unfortunately the cartridges were notoriously fickle and the brass rims kept jamming as did the breech when the rifle overheated in battle. They were fine for the Zulu Wars when most Zulus wielded assegais, but were now slightly out of date.

Kruger realised that they had to get the latest weapons if they were to stand any chance of winning the war, and fast. The Martini-Henry was fine for Majuba in 1881 but the young Boers, like de La Rey, Botha, de Wet and Jan Smuts, were champing at the bit. The Germans were on hand and negotiated a deal. In 1896 the Boers ordered 70,000 Mauser rifles and carbines from Ludwig Loewe, whose firm was later known as Deutsche Waffen- und Munitionfabriken (DWM). Of these only about 55,000 ever got there due to the sea blockade. There were other rifles from Austria but the Mauser soon became the weapon of choice.

The calibre of the Mauser was 7 mm, it had an effective range of over 2,000 yards, some even reached 3,500 yards. They were accurate, fast firing and very handy for horsemen and mounted infantry. They cost about £3 each and the ammunition was £6 a thousand. Smokeless powder, invented by the French, was invaluable when fighting a guerrilla war or any other war for that matter. Some commandos carried two bandoliers

Lt Percy Evans-Freke with pipe and Sgt Major Ewart with binos and men on Tiger's Kloof. © Leicestershire Yeomanry
(Sadly Lt Col Percy Evans-Freke was killed defending a trench during The Battle of Second Ypres in May 1915)

which meant 120 rounds. Good for a shoot out.

Whilst slow off the mark for the Mauser, Piet managed to negotiate a deal for some of the latest artillery pieces available. From Krupps in Essen he ordered eight x 75 mm field guns Q.F. and four 120 mm howitzers. From the French armaments firm Schneider et Cie at Le Creusot he ordered six of their latest 75 mm Q.F. field guns. It was the first field gun to include a hydro-pneumatic recoil mechanism, which kept the gun's trail and wheels perfectly still during the firing sequence and meant that it did not have to be re-aimed before every shot. Q.F. meant Quick Firing and a good crew could fire fifteen rounds per minute on its target, either shrapnel or high-explosive. Range up to about five miles and some crews even managed 30 rounds a minute. But the Boers had to make every shell count. The British version of high explosive was called Lyddite. A secret name derived from it place of manufacture: Lydd in Kent.

Joubert also ordered from Creusot, four of their latest 155 mm heavy guns which delivered a shell that weighed nearly a cwt over a range of 9,000 yards and was later called the 'Long Tom'. Joubert bought 8,880 rounds. He also wisely bought some of the latest Maxim Nordenfelt heavy duty machine guns which could fire 600 explosive shells per minute and was accurate at 1,200 yards. They were water cooled. The British had turned them down but soon changed their mind when the war started and their version was made at Vickers Armstrong in Elswick, Newcastle upon Tyne.

At the Siege of Ladysmith one of these howitzers was named *Slim Piet*, and was sited on Umbulwane. In late November 1899 during a raid south of the Tugela river in Natal, Piet Joubert was thrown from his horse and

Maxim Nordenfeld – the Pom-Pom

suffered internal injuries. He died on 28 March 1900. He was very reluctant to go to war mainly because he had seen it all before and knew in his bones that the British Army would win in the end. Other younger more fiery generals took over. Piet Joubert was greatly respected by General Sir George White, the defender of Ladysmith, as he had allowed the women and children to leave when the siege started and also allowed the setting up of a hospital in a neutral zone for all their casualties, on one condition: that they did not return. Sir George White called Piet Joubert 'a soldier and a gentleman, and a brave and honourable opponent'. Even Rudyard Kipling wrote a poem upon his death, 'Piet Joubert', absolving him from complicity in instigating the war. Slim Piet was an astute but reluctant general.

However Piet Joubert's nephew, Fritz Joubert Duquesne was a very different kettle of fish. He went to university in London and the Belgian Military Academy.

General Joubert and his staff having lunch at Newcastle

During the Boer War he was wounded at the Siege of Ladysmith, having served with the artillery. He then made his way to England in 1901 and apparently enlisted under a false name to become a British army officer. He was however caught as a spy and lucky not to have been executed by the British. The other twenty members of his sabotage team in Cape Town were executed. He was sent to a prison camp in Bermuda and was always trying to escape.

Duquesne, a rebel with a cause, bitterly resented the treatment of the women and children in the British concentration camps where his mother and sister had both died. After the war he became a big game hunter, war correspondent, journalist and fraudster. He even became Theodore Roosevelt's personal shooting instructor. But he was very restless.

During the First War he worked in Brazil as a German spy and he planted time bombs disguised as cases of mineral samples on British ships; he was credited with sinking twenty-two ships. He even claimed that he had helped sink *H.M.S Hampshire* which sank with Kitchener onboard. But this, as with so much else about his life, was pure fantasy.

His grudge against Britain also extended to the Second World War when he ran a large spy ring in the United States relaying secret information on Allied weaponry and shipping movements to Germany. The Duquesne Gang which was composed of thirty men and three women was rounded up by the F.B.I. in June 1941. The gang were all given lengthy sentences totalling 300 years which pretty well scuppered Germany's intelligence gathering in the United States for the rest of the war.

During the trial, Duquesne, claimed that his actions were aimed at Britain as revenge for the crimes done to his people and his country during the Second Anglo-Boer War. He served thirteen years of his eighteen year sentence in prison and was released on grounds of ill health. Fritz Joubert Duquesne later died in hospital on Roosevelt Island, New York in 1956 at the age of 78.

So the effects of the Boer War lived on for many years. Not sure if his pious uncle Slim Piet would have approved of his colourful lifestyle.

Last Chance Saloon
Bloemfontein 31 May – 5 June 1899

This important meeting in Bloemfontein which started on 31 May 1899 had been arranged by Martinus Steyn who was President of the Orange Free State. He had studied law and had been called to the Bar at the Inner Temple. It was the last real chance to avert war, which started five months later in October 1899. The issues were complicated, but in the wake of the Jameson Raid three years earlier, Kruger knew full well which way the wind was blowing. The raid backed by Rhodes and Beit, and even secretly by Joe Chamberlain, left no doubt about the British intentions or their ability to provide trumped up excuses for intervention in the affairs of the Transvaal. They also wanted to get their hands on the gold fields.

Sir Alfred Milner was an acute administrator and had been a friend of the economic historian Arnold Toynbee at Balliol. Sir Alfred had also been brought up in the Grand Duchy of Hesse in Germany. His grandmother was German and his father was a doctor and Reader in English at Tubingen University. Sir Alfred saw the British

The Bloemfontein Conference – Reception at the Presidency
Sir Alfred Milner meets President Kruger

as the 'superior race' and did not really hide his dislike of the Afrikaners. Kruger who was married and had seventeen children knew full well what war meant and simply said with tears in his eyes 'It is our country you want'. The odds were always against the Boers. Their population was very small when pitted against the might of the British Empire but they knew their country very well and had enough men and Mausers to catch the British napping, which in the end is exactly what they did.

Jan Smuts was very astute as always. To say that Sir Alfred Milner was 'more dangerous than Cecil Rhodes' was very perceptive. The six day conference wore Sir Alfred out and in the end he simply drew stumps, called an end to play in a very undiplomatic way and walked off the pitch. He closed the conference with the words. 'This conference is absolutely at an end, and there is no obligation on either side arising from it.' He had no desire for compromise. Troops were already being sent from India and Britain. The sabre rattling had begun. In fact it had been going on for years.

If the talks had been successful and there were clear indications that they could have been, even on the thorny subjects of Uitlanders and their franchise, voting rights and the number of seats in parliament, then the Boer War could have been prevented and many thousands of innocent lives spared.

Sir Alfred was keen to get back to Cape Town as he had just started an affair with the wife of an army officer – Lady Violet Georgina Gascoyne-Cecil whom he eventually married in 1921. Sir Alfred, later Lord Milner, died of sleeping sickness which he had contracted from being bitten by a *tsetse* fly whilst on a short visit to South Africa in 1925. One of his best known protégés was John Buchan, author of *Thirty-Nine Steps* and *Greenmantle*.

Ultimatum

This was delivered on 9 October 1899 from Paul Kruger to the British Government and expired after forty-eight hours. It was not exactly a declaration of war itself, but merely stated that it recognised the warlike intentions of Great Britain if the points were not adhered to. In other words if Britain does not back off and withdraw her troops from the Transvaal borders she would suffer the consequences. A tall order. Milner was miffed. In the Foreign Office back in London some of the officials laughed. But very soon they had the smiles and smirks wiped off their faces as the casualty figures mounted. What to them might have seemed a joke at the time was in fact deadly serious. The Empire was swiftly thrown into chaos. The wording of Kruger's Ultimatum ran like this:

(a) That all points of mutual difference shall be regulated by the friendly course of arbitration or by whatever amicable way may be agreed upon by this Government with Her Majesty's Government.

(b) That the troops on the borders of this Republic shall be instantly withdrawn.

(c) That all reinforcements of troops which have arrived in South Africa since the 1st June, 1899, shall be removed from South Africa within a reasonable time, to be agreed upon with this Government, and with a mutual assurance and guarantee on the part of this Government that no attack upon or hostilities against any portion of the possessions of the British Government shall be made by the Republic during further negotiations within a period of time to be subsequently agreed upon between the Governments, and this Government will, on compliance therewith, be prepared to withdraw the armed burghers of this Republic from the borders.

(d) That Her Majesty's troops which are now on the high seas shall not be landed in any port of South Africa.

This Government must press for an immediate and affirmative answer to these four questions, and earnestly requests Her Majesty's Government to return such an answer before or upon Wednesday the 11th October, 1899, not later than 5 o'clock p.m., and it desires further to add that in the event of unexpectedly no satisfactory answer being received by it within that interval it will with great regret be compelled to regard the action of Her Majesty's Government as a formal declaration of war, and will not hold itself responsible for the consequences thereof, and that in the event of any further movements of troops taking place within the above-mentioned time in the nearer directions of our borders this Government will be compelled to regard that also as a formal declaration of war.

Ferreira, Jumper, Bonanza and Robinson Deep are all well known gold mines on the Rand. Those Uitlanders who wanted to side with the British legged it to Natal. Those that sided with the Boers stayed put and found a commando to their liking. Others wisely vanished.

The Reply

Self evident but not exactly a declaration of war either. It seems as if both sides slipped into war without really realising what was going on. Many of the Boer generals were very reluctant and had only stocked up with arms to be on the defensive. They puffed their pipes and read their Bibles.

Sharks – The Passage Out

Once the war had started and the press had whipped the public into a frenzy, thousands upon thousands of young men volunteered. Not so much for the regular army but for the glamour of the Colonial and Imperial Yeomanry units that were often used as mounted infantry.

There were many gentleman troopers who served in the ranks even in regular units. Men came from all over the Empire: Canada, New South Wales, Tasmania and New Zealand, even ships crews deserted and went inland. At five shillings a day you were on good money, but the work was both arduous and dangerous. The Boers were fighting on their home territory.

Troopship – The calm before the storm

The voice of Trooper Theodore Vandermere Fleming is typical and phlegmatic. I interviewed him when he was in his nineties in Bexhill-on-Sea. For him it was as if the Boer War was only yesterday. He had deep respect for the Boers and later went on to serve as an officer in the First and Second World Wars. His elder brother worked in the War Office. Theodore was very good with horses and mules. More about Bethune's Mounted Infantry later.

Capture of *Mosquito*

Otherwise known as the Battle of Kraaipan. This was a small affair involving an armoured train called *Mosquito*, carrying two seven-pounder cannons, rifles and much ammunition. It was commanded by Lieutenant R.H. Nesbitt and fifteen men of the Bechuanaland Protectorate Field Force as well as a skilled telegraphist. But as the telephone lines had been cut the telegraphist was out of a job and had to pick up a rifle. These were in fact the first shots of the Boer War – 12 October 1899. The Ultimatum had expired at 5.30 p.m. the day before, so

Wrecking the armoured train at Kraaipan

war had only just officially been declared.

After a Bible reading session 800 Boers of the Potchefstroom and Lichtenburg commandos under Generals Koos de la Rey and Piet Cronjé surrounded a small British garrison and railway siding at Kraaipan about thirty-five miles south west of Mafeking. The armoured train went ahead even though warned of the Boer presence and was derailed and ambushed. The railway lines had been cut and removed to one side.

The battle went on all night as the British tried to get the train back on the rails but by the morning the crew were heavily outnumbered and surrounded. They were held down by artillery and the train received a direct hit on its boiler sending steam everywhere. Their situation became hopeless so they raised the white flag and became the first British prisoners of the war. Several men were wounded but contrary to first reports no one was killed on either side. As always the first casualty in war was truth.

Whilst escaping from Mafeking Lady Sarah Wilson heard the battle in the distance and later saw the train, which was then surrounded by a swarm of locusts. Vellum was her faithful Zulu servant.

Lady Sarah Wilson (1865-1929) otherwise known as Lady Sarah Isabella Augusta Spencer-Churchill was an intrepid and very attractive young lady married to an officer in the Household Cavalry – Captain Gordon Wilson, who was A.D.C. to Colonel Baden-Powell in Mafeking.

Aged 34 she was also Winston Churchill's aunt and only nine years older than him, Randolph Churchill being her elder brother. She became one of the world's first women war correspondents. When the *Daily Mail* correspondent Ralph Hellawell was arrested by the Boers for trying to smuggle one of his dispatches out of town,

Lady Sarah Wilson

Lady Sarah was asked by Alfred Harmsworth to cover the Siege of Mafeking for the *Daily Mail*. Although technically untrained in the dark arts of journalism she became a war reporter, a task which she undertook with great style and alacrity.

Interestingly in 1881 another woman writer, Lady Florence Dixie covered the First Boer War as a field correspondent for *The Morning Post* and even interviewed Cetshwayo when he was captured. *The Morning Post* was the same newspaper that Winston Churchill worked for.

Shrapnel House underground café, Kimberley

Signalling

This account of officers signalling with pocket watch cases was recounted to me by Trooper Theodore Fleming of Bethune's Mounted Infantry. The morse message at the beginning of the poem spells out 'Boer War'. Conventional British Army heliographs had 3-inch, 5-inch and 10-inch mirrors and skilled signallers could manage speeds of up to sixteen words per minute. The beam was very narrow, spreading only 50 feet per mile of range. The maximum range was considered to be 10 miles for each inch of mirror diameter. It could however

Heliograph master class

also be read by the enemy if they were in direct line of sight. The heliograph in most general use was that of Mr Henry Mance, of the Government Persian Gulf Telegraph Department; but an 'improved' instrument had been constructed by Captain Begbie, of the Madras Engineers. The Mance instrument, or 'Field Heliograph', consisted of a small 4.5 inch mirror. In excellent conditions the heliograph had a range of nearly 100 miles.

The Boers also used heliographs to keep in touch with their outlying commandos. The heliograph was so useful that it was even used in the Western Desert in the Second World War by South African and Australian units, where radio silence was a distinct advantage.
Heliographs were also used on the North-West Frontier and by Afghan forces during the Soviet Invasion of Afghanistan in the 1980s. Intelligence and discrete signalling were always highly prized. It gave your forces a certain advantage and flexibility... so long as the sun was shining.

Hedgehog

The war was only four days old and everyone was feeling their way. No one quite knew what was happening. Lt. Francis Maxwell Chevenix Trench was in 69th Field Battery Royal Artillery based at the coal mining town of Dundee in Natal. Coal was important for the steam locomotives. Max Chevenix Trench like his brother Christopher kept diaries often in letter form and whenever they could, they sent them back to their parents Colonel Charles Trench & Mrs Emily Trench. As a boy Colonel Trench had seen the funeral of Wellington and had met several of the veterans of Waterloo. His wife called Emily Lefroy, was the daughter of Major General John Lefroy, well known for his surveys in Canada and studies in magnetism. He also corresponded at length with Florence Nightingale about army reform. A strong military family in other words.

Max survived the war even though he was banged up in Ladysmith. His brother Christoper did not, he died of enteric fever in Bloemfontein.

Spies

Mapping was a major problem as the maps were not the best. The Boers also had to quickly find out where the British forces were and what sort of men they were up against. Spies were common on both sides. History does not relate what happened to these two men. They could have been shot, captured or simply escaped. They were obviously up to no good. Max Chevenix Trench saw action a few days later at the Battle of Talana.

Mark Twain on the Boer War

The first quote is taken from a letter written about the Boer War by Mark Twain to his friend the Rev. Joe Twichell in December 1899.

Boer messengers under armed guard and blindfolded near Paardeberg February 1900

The second quote is from a letter to William Dean Howells, 25 January 1900.

The third quote is when Mark Twain introduced Winston Churchill to a packed audience at the Grand Ballroom of the Waldorf-Astoria, New York on 12 December 1900. Mark Twain was appalled at the Boer War and the way that it had started but also realised that England and America were closely allied. As he also said in his introductory remarks about England: 'We have always been kin: kin in blood, kin in religion, kin in representative government, kin in ideals, kin in just and lofty purposes; and now we are kin in sin, the harmony is complete, the blend is perfect, like Mr. Churchill himself, whom I now have the honor to present to you'.

Mr Churchill was talking about his escape from Pretoria, where he was held in a converted school.

Coffee with the Boers

This episode occurred when Lady Sarah was being held under a form of house arrest and was waiting to be taken to the Boer general in his laager.

At the outbreak of war, Baden-Powell had asked Lady Sarah Wilson to leave the town as he was afraid for her safety and heard that there were 8,000 Boers planning an immediate assault. She then left her husband and travelled at night through enemy countryside with her maid, a Cape cart, some mules and a Zulu called Vellum. She was supposed to go to the Kalahari but ended up in a small hotel with a store at Setlagoli 35 miles south in Bechuanaland, on the main road to Kimberley. Whilst travelling at night she heard artillery shots coming from the Battle of Kraaipan.

Lady Sarah Wilson

Lady Sarah stayed at Setlagoli for a month or more. Occasionally it was just possible to get messages in and out of Mafeking and native guides were very canny at getting through Boer lines. One trusted man named Boaz carried small notes hidden in a cartridge case and was paid £3 for each trip he made. A very good wage but if he had been caught he would almost certainly have been executed.

One day Mr 'P' from Reuters also turned up at Setlagoli and he had a few homing pigeons. He wrote a note to Baden-Powell saying where Lady Sarah was and that she was willing to act as an intermediary for getting any information either into or out of Mafeking. This was risky to say the least. Never trust a journalist. Pigeons seemed so much safer than risking the lives of trusted loyal couriers. Never trust a pigeon...

The pigeon circled round and round for twenty minutes then flew off. In fact it flew not to Makefing but straight to a Boer laager, perched on the general's roof and was promptly shot and no doubt eaten. The Boers read the message and went out looking for the 'spy' Lady Sarah. She was found and kept under house arrest for a few days. A little irritated and because the food was starting to run out, she then demanded a meeting with

Louis Botha and Mrs Botha

the Boer generals and asked to be sent back to join her husband in Mafeking.

General Snyman and Commandant Botha were very suspicious of her and she was kept under armed guard in the squalid operating theatre of a local hospital. Eventually after some bargaining she was returned to Mafeking and exchanged for a well known horse thief called Petrus Viljoen, not to be confused with the Boer general Ben Viljoen, his grandfather!

Lady Sarah then rejoined her husband and Baden-Powell in the garrison and commenced a more or less underground existence, as she saw out the Siege of Mafeking which lasted for another five and a half months, right through till 17 May 1900. She also worked as a nurse and later wrote up her experiences in a book called *South African Memories* which was published in 1909.

Twee tozen Engelman dood means two thousand Englishmen dead not two dozen… referring either to the Battle of Modder River – or possibly Magersfontein – casualty figures which were greatly exaggerated.

Are there any Boers about?

Part 3

Getting
Stuck In

On Patrol

Went out in fours –
Reconnaissance they called it.
And when it came to a shoot out
Number three held the horses –
Soon got wise to that one.

Colonel Bethune – On patrol

Patrolling for weeks on end
One major wouldn't let us dismount,
So when we came under fire,
They were falling from the saddle
He didn't last long – Silly bugger.

Just like hunting back home –
Picking up the scent, sniffing the wind
Reading the spoors, looking for water.
Never did trust the farmhouses.
Even orchards could be a death trap.

Trooper Theodore Fleming
Bethune's Mounted Infantry

Boers in British cavalry cloaks entrap a patrol

Battle of Talana

I

The horses had all just been unhooked
When we heard guns fired and shells
Started to plump into the lines all over the place.

In a very short time we had hooked in and limbered up.
There was some slight confusion among the horses,
But the men were all as cool and steady as at any other time

And behaved splendidly. Half a dozen loose horses
Galloping about in the lines, frightened of course
By the shell, singing about all around them.

We went over the railway in battery column
Got the order 'Sections left wheel and Action Front'
The enemy's guns opened fire on the camp at 5.45

And we started on them at 6.20. They soon got
Our range, but the range was a bit long for them,
And they only got timed shrapnel into us.

When we got into them we pounded away
At battery fire 10 or 15 seconds, for some little time.
All this while we were at limber supply...

So the limber numbers were kept very busy
As they had to supply ammunition and fuze shells
At the same time. However we never ran short.

They did not do us much harm, killing
One trumpeter and putting a splinter through
The hand of one of my No.1's – Sergeant Lindfield.

He did not seem much hurt and carried on all right
Till Doctor Major took him away. Everyone
Is awfully sorry about the trumpeter, Horn.

He was the youngest in the Brigade Division.
16 years old, and they very nearly sent him down
To Pietermaritzburg with the boys of the 18th Hussars.

II

We then limbered up and went on again
Through the town to a second position.
About 1,600 yards ahead was a big wood

And a house or two, near the foot of the hill
Where we could see the infantry collecting
For the attack. On our left were the 18th,

On our right the Mounted Infantry. Just behind us
The town of Dundee. The rifle fire in this wood
Was very rapid indeed, and a lot of them were plugging away

At us from long range with Mausers.
There were no end of shots dropping all around us
But no harm was done to men or horses here.

As their artillery fire had stopped, we shelled the ridge
Of the hill all along wherever we could see groups
Of men moving about and gave it to them very hot.

While we were in action the townspeople
Were awfully kind to us, they brought
Us out cocoa, bread and water,

Which were very welcome
As we had had no breakfast
Beyond a cup of tea before coming out.

III

About 11 o'clock Colonel Hammersley
Came back with the news that the General had been shot
And would be out of action for the rest of the day.

Hammersley said the fire from the top of the hill
Into the wood was the hottest he had ever seen.
There was a continuous rattle of musketry

And they sent a lot of rifle bullets singing round us too.
We advanced about 900 or 1,000 yards at a fast trot
Under a heavy fire from their rifle men,

Who did little damage to us. They hit three or four horses
And grazed three men, one got a bullet through the shoulder.
Both batteries gave them a few minutes of battery fire

At 10 seconds and 5 seconds and in some
Ten minutes or so they had entirely ceased firing on us.
We saw them running away on top of the hill

In all directions while the infantry rushed up the crest.
It was an extraordinary sight.
All sorts of Boer ponies had been captured,

And several prisoners taken.
We got into camp late, in the dark
And left our harness on the horses.

Lt Max Chevenix Trench Friday 20 October 1899

*Cape Garrison Artillery making it hot for the Boers
across the Modder River*

Lancers

Two men being killed on one horse
Seems rather a tall order,
Yet it is perfectly true.
It happened at the cavalry charge after Elandslaagte.

Some of the Boers stood their ground
With great stubbornness
Till our cavalry were only a few yards away.

One middle-aged, bearded fellow
Stayed just a little too long,
And had not time to get to his horse,
Which was a few yards away.

He scrambled up behind a brother Boer
Who was just mounting, but almost immediately
The 5th Lancers were upon them.

There was a farrier-corporal,
An immensely big, powerful fellow,
Who singled them out.

They were galloping down a slight incline
As hard as they could get their horse to travel,
But their pursuer was gaining on them at every stride.

When he came within striking distance
He jammed his spurs into his big horse,
Who sprang forward like a tiger.
Weight of man and horse, impetus of gallop and hill,
Focused in that bright lance-point held as in a vice.

It pierced the left side of
The back of the man behind,
And the point came out through the right
Side of the man in front,
Who, with a convulsive movement, threw up
His hands, flinging his rifle in the air.

The Lancer could not
Withdraw his lance as the men swayed
And dropped from their horse, but
Galloped on into the gathering darkness
Punctured with rifle flashes here and there
And flitting forms that might be friend or foe.

This poor fellow was killed a few days after
At the Battle of Rietfontein.

How heartily the Boers hated these Lancers!

George Lynch
Troops: 5th Royal Irish Lancers and 5th Dragoons

Battle of Modder River

Old McCormick was half the problem
Burns the backs of your knees.

'Glorious, brilliant, summer morning it was
Like walking up on a grouse moor.'

They promised us breakfast when we got to the river.
Some sort of hotel supposed to be there

A few rowing boats tucked away in the willows –
A bit like Henley-on-Thames.

'They're not here.' the General said
'They're sitting uncommonly tight if they are.' Colville replied,

Roughing it by the Modder River – Officers' mess 3rd Grenadier Guards

Crossing the Modder River. This bridge was built in two hours by 7 Field Company Royal Engineers 1900

Red dust danced in front of our eyes – red dust
And sand – had us fooled, we paid the price.

'Very unsporting this smokeless powder'
Must have seen us coming for miles and miles

Didn't stand a chance – couldn't advance
Exotic butterflies pinned down on the veldt

Held their fire – 1,000 yards
Murder it was – the ants were bad.

Couldn't move an inch, or even a hand
Even a thistle – good cover for the damned

Ten hours we lay there under the sun
Lips cracked – tongues swollen – kilts awry.

Others crawled back for water, they were shot.
A curse on this land for being so hot

The sound of battle – strange indeed
'Like ripping cloth, the tearing of the air'.

'Like the crackle of a piece of gorse in a blazing fire'.
Or 'the perpetual frying of fat'

As thousands of Mausers
Blazed and bubbled away

'The air was humming and throbbing,
And the sand mottled like a pond in shower. '

'Now and again there came the dull thud
Of a bullet which had found its mark,

And a man gasped, or drummed with his feet'
Others smoked pipes or fell asleep

All day we lay under a blistering sun,
The 'sleet of bullets whizzing over our heads'.

'It came in solid streaks like telegraph wires',
Said one correspondent behind the lines.

Men lay on their rifles to keep them cool
And then the artillery had us in range.

'We learnt afterwards that Major Albrecht
Had trained in Prussia and knew his job very well.'

'Like Dante's inferno' the General said
Writing back to his wife Mary Ethel

'Third battle in a week' – then the sun went down
We buried the dead. The Boers fled.

Slag van die Twee Riviere
'They're not here.' the General said

Promised us breakfast when we got to the river.
Red dust danced in front of our eyes.

Modder River village after artillery bombardment

Kilts

The highland kilt
Was not really designed
With this sort of war
And the Boers in mind,

For the sporran you see
Gives long range snipers
A very unfair advantage –
A bit below the belt.

We had many stomach wounds
So they gave us aprons,
Khaki of course,
That we put on in front.

Camouflage of the aforesaid sporran
Ditched the spats,
Unpolished our buttons,
Swords and claymores sent packing

Warfare ancient and modern

Argyll & Sutherland Highlanders setting out on patrol.
Note the khaki aprons covering up kilts and sporrans.

Bayonet sheaths toned down.
No glint, no hint, no sign of rank
Officers looked as rough as we did.
And took it on the chin

Pith helmet and slouch hat.
Take your pick.
Farewell badger skin.
But the barbed wire was our undoing.

Corporal James MacDonald Mackay Argyll & Sutherland Highlanders
playing 'The Campbells are Coming'
to rally the soldiers at the Battle of Magersfontein

Battle of Magersfontein
11 December 1899

Two short extracts from two differing versions by an anonymous soldier in the 2nd Black Watch.
– 'One Who was There'.

I The Cape Town Version

Tell you a tale of a battle
Well, there ain't so much to tell.
Nine hundred marched to the slaughter
And nigh on four hundred fell.
Wire and the mauser rifle
Thirst and a burning sun
Brought us down by the hundred
Ere that black day was done.
Someone yelled charge and we started.
Rose and rushed out on their fire
Meaning to give them the bayonet
But checked and stopped by barbed wire
Bullets and shells never appalled us
Trenches nor boulder strewn hill
But just a few strands of wire fencing
Brought us non-plussed standing still.
'Over the wire men or through it'
'Drive the charge home to the hill'
Vain were our struggles and climbing
Deep stuck the barbs in our kilts.

II The Johannesburg Version

Down on the face and seek cover
Nothing could live in that fire
'Off to the right men and flank them'
Forward, lie down men – retire.

Why weren't we told of the trenches?
Why weren't we told of the wire?
Why were we marching in column?
May Tommy Atkins enquire.

Boer trenches at Modder River

Block House mentality - Princess Louise's A&S Highlanders

*South African Light Horse on patrol
with ostrich feathers in their slouch hats*

Why were no scouts sent on forward?
Why were no scouts on our flank?
We attacked in quarter column
Who made the mistake give his rank.

Do they know this in Old England?
Do they know this incompetence yet
Tommy has learnt to his sorrow
And Tommy will never forget.

Such was the day for our Regiment
Dread the revenge we will take.
Dearly we paid for the blunder
A drawing room General's mistake.

Barbed Wire Debate

I

There was an ordinary wire fence
on the farm of Magersfontein,
but it had been there for years,

and was intended to enclose a sheep
and cattle ranch, and not to serve
as part of a plan of battle.

This boundary fence played nothing
save an accidental part
in the events of the 11th of December.

Michael Davitt reporting from the Boer side

II

It matters not what gave the signal,
whether it was the flashing of a lantern by a Boer scout,
or the tripping of a soldier over wire,
or the firing of a gun in the ranks.

It may have been any,
or it may have been none, of these things.
As a matter of fact I have been
assured by a Boer who was present
that it was the sound of the tins

attached to the alarm wires
which disturbed them.

Some, the most unfortunate of all,
became caught in the darkness
in the wire defences,
and were found in the morning
hung up 'like crows',
as one spectator describes it,
and riddled with bullets.

Arthur Conan Doyle reporting on the British side

Barbed wire at Magersfontein. This was a formidable obstacle when under intense fire. Shades of things to come in 1914.

Death from a Mauser Bullet

Death from a Mauser bullet is less painful
than the drawing of a tooth. Such, at least,
appears to be the case, speaking generally
from apparent evidence, without having
the opportunity of collecting the opinions
of those who have actually died.

The first man I saw badly hit during the war
was a Devon at Elandslaagte,
just after they had advanced within rifle-range.
He was shot through the head,
and it seemed quite useless for the bearers
to take the trouble of carrying him off the field;
yet they went back looking in vain for a field ambulance.

They carried him instead to the cart belonging
to a well-known war correspondent.
The owner had given the driver strict orders
to remain where he was until his return,
but the shells were falling around the cart,
which, in fact, seemed to be made a mark of
by the Boer gunners – perhaps they thought
it belonged to one of our generals,
whom they may have imagined had taken to driving,
like Joubert and some others of theirs.

The arrival of the wounded man
was a great godsend to the driver,
who immediately, with the most humane insistence,
offered to drive him to the nearest field hospital.
Neither cart nor driver was again seen
until long after the battle was over,
about nine o'clock in the evening.
Strange to say, the man recovered from his wound.

George Lynch

George Lynch – War correspondent

Dum-Dum

Captain Neville Sneyd Bertie-Clay
Invented the Dum-Dum bullet one day
For use on the North-West Frontier
And other small colonial wars
That were fast becoming running sores.

Dum Dum, near Calcutta in Bengal
No Tigers now – where the airport is today –
Arsenal and chief munitions factory.
Deolali by the way is near Bombay –
In case your mind is blown away.

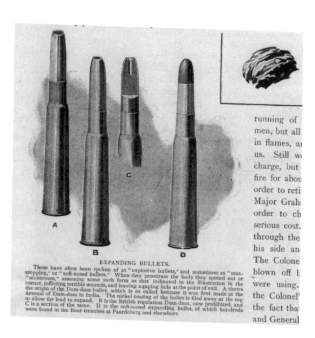

EXPANDING BULLETS.

These have often been spoken of as "explosive bullets," and sometimes as "man-stopping," or "soft-nosed bullets." When they penetrate the body they spread out or "mushroom," assuming some such form as that indicated in the illustration in the corner, inflicting terrible wounds, and leaving a gaping hole at the point of exit. A shows the origin of the Dum-dum bullet, which is so called because it was first made at the Arsenal of Dum-dum in India. The nickel coating of the bullet is filed away at the top to allow the lead to expand. B is the British regulation Dum dum, now prohibited, and C is a section of the same. D is the soft-nosed expanding bullet, of which hundreds were found in the Boer trenches at Paardeberg and elsewhere.

running of
men, but all
in flames, a
us. Still w
charge, but
fire for abou
order to reti
Major Grah
order to ch
serious cost.
through the
his side an
The Colone
blown off k
were using.
the Colonel'
the fact tha
and General

'You see these newer, smaller, lighter, faster bullets
Drill neat little holes in a man,
But don't stop him charging downhill.
You need something, a bit more expansive,
To slow him up, if you get my drift.'

So the bullets were altered. 'Mark IV & Mark V
To be precise – Lee Metford – Lee Enfield
Mark my word – Quite a rifle – 303 no less
Just the nickel sheath stripped back a bit.'
To show the dull grey tip of lead, its deadly eye

That could explode and rip a man in half.
So when the Boer War began to flare
Both sides accused each other of their use.
Even a war correspondent lost an arm
Which made the point – they cause a lot of harm.

Young Churchill had a clip or two about his person
When caught beside the armoured train.
'A souvenir of Omdurman.' He said he'd picked them up
Upon the battle field, disposed of them discreetly.
Lucky man, the Boers looked the other way.

And as for Captain Neville Sneyd Bertie-Clay
He served his time, made Colonel on the way
Quietly retired to the South Sea Isles
Tahiti to be precise which I am told is very nice
He only died a year before the Second War.

Truce at Magersfontein

In the intervals of armistice
which were subsequently arranged,
the enemy behaved with great courtesy.

They had given water to our wounded
of the Highland Brigade
early in the morning after the battle.

These poor fellows had lain all day Monday
under heavy fire and hot sun,
and all Monday night, which was particularly cold,
without water, and they had had no food
since Sunday evening.

The Boer Commander, General Cronjé,
was exceedingly courteous and kind,
assisting in every way possible.
He further offered fifty burghers
To help to bury our dead.

Lord Methuen sent a letter of thanks
to General Cronjé for his courtesy.

The London Standard **war correspondent**

Often the wounded had to be carried off the battle field under fire

Horsedrawn field ambulance South African Light Horse

Burial Parties

The English dead were very badly buried,
and General Cronjé had to communicate
with Lord Methuen on Wednesday
to point out that the work was so hastily done
that limbs were protruding from the too shallow pits
in which the bodies had been interred.

I was solemnly assured by the Rev. Mr Marquardt,
of the Dutch Reformed Church, who was present
during the scene, which he described with a shudder,
that the second burial party sent by Methuen
were all intoxicated while performing
the gruesome task of re-burying their comrades.

Drink was, it appears, deemed to be necessary
for the burying party, owing to the rapid decomposition
of the bodies after lying some days in the broiling sun.
Some of the Tommies jumped on the covering of the pits
so as to press down the bulging carcases of the dead.

A horrible and sickening scene, truly;
but it is only by the painting of war in its true
and ghastly character, and not in its tinsel trappings,
that the victims of war – the working men –
may be induced not to lend their support
to those who wage war for other
than noble and patriotic ends.

Michael Davitt

You could hear nothing
But the wailing of the pibrochs
As the Highlanders were buried.

A Colour-Sergeant of the 2nd Black Watch

Intombi cemetery Ladysmith.
The two crosses nearest are sailors from HMS Powerful *who died*
during the siege: P. H. Newman and Hans A. Lister.

When the Balloon Goes Up

Ghostly the silent sphere,
Rises slowly behind the lines
The uneasy air of quiet observation
Towed behind lumbering ox wagons.

Men holding ropes, the rigmarole about to escalate
Where men in their baskets
Wield their fiendish telescopes and make notes

84th Battery R.A. and Balloon Corps

As if they are out mapping
At home on their country estates,
Take the first aerial photographs ever.
But we know better,
It is terribly unsporting to spy on your neighbour
Even though he may have
DUG A FEW EXTRA TRENCHES IN THE NIGHT
And moved his guns around.

'We would never do such a thing? would we?'

'Do you call this fair play
That damnable round thing
Spying on our positions?'

Well we will fool you all the same
And only get into position at night.
And wait for you and by dawn
When you have had your breakfast
We will be well back behind our lines.
So when the balloon goes up
We know full well what is coming our way.

'Captain Jones is on the blower Sir.'

Paul Kruger, you know, he went up in a balloon
When he visited Paris twenty years ago.
It's all hot air and hydrogen to me.

Let's take a pot shot.

Conan Doyle on Colenso

On approaching the Drift – the position
or even the existence of which does not seem
to have been very clearly defined –

it was found that the troops had to advance
into a loop formed by the river,
so that they were exposed to a very heavy cross-fire

upon their right flank, while they were rained on
by shrapnel from in front. No sign of the enemy
could be seen, though the men were dropping fast.

It is a weird and soul-shaking experience to advance
over a sunlit and apparently lonely countryside,
with no slightest movement upon its broad face,

while the path which you take is marked behind you
by sobbing, gasping, writhing men,
who can only guess by the position of their wounds

whence the shots came which struck them down.
All round, like the hissing of fat in the pan,
is the monotonous crackle and rattle of the Mausers;

but the air is full of it, and no one can define exactly
whence it comes. Far away on some hill
upon the skyline there hangs the least gauzy veil

of thin smoke to indicate whence the six men
who have just all fallen together,
as if it were some grim drill, met their death.

Into such a hell-storm as this it was
that the soldiers have again and again
advanced in the course of this war,

but it may be questioned whether they will not
prove to be among the last of mortals
to be asked to endure such an ordeal.

Other methods of attack must be found or attacks
must be abandoned, for smokeless powder, quick-firing guns,
and modern rifles make it all odds on the defence!

*Dash of the 2nd Royal Dublin Fusiliers across the Tugela River
Battle of Colenso 15 December 1899*

Mahatma Gandhi at Spion Kop

'My first meeting with Mr M. Gandhi
was under strange circumstances.
It was on the road from Spion Kop,
after the fateful retirement
of the British troops in January 1900.

The previous afternoon I saw
the Indian mule-train moved up the slopes
of the Kop carrying water to the distressed soldiers
who had lain powerless on the plateau.

The mules carried the water in immense bags,
one on each side, led by Indians at their heads.

The galling rifle-fire, which heralded their arrival
on the top, did not deter the strangely-looking cavalcade
which moved slowly forward, and as an Indian fell,
another quietly stepped forward to fill the vacant place.

Afterwards the grim duty of bearer corps,
which Mr Gandhi organised in Natal, began.

After a night's work, which had shattered men
with much bigger frames
I came across Gandhi in the early morning
sitting by the roadside, eating a regulation army biscuit.

Every man in Buller's force was dull and depressed,
and damnation was heartily invoked on everything.

But Gandhi was stoical in his bearing,
cheerful, and confident in his conversation,
and had a kindly eye. He did one good...

I saw the man and his small undisciplined corps
on many a field during the Natal campaign.
When succour was to be rendered they were there.'

Vere Palgrave Stent

*Stretcher-bearers of the Indian Ambulance Corps during the war,
including the future leader Mohandas Karamchand Gandhi (Middle
row, 5th from left). He is sitting next to Dr Lancelot Booth who helped
Gandhi raise and train the Ambulance Corps.*

Slightly Wounded

A technical phrase you might think
But it is often a medical master of understatement.
'For instance here in Pietermaritzburg
We have one Private Brown of the Northumberlands

Cheerful lad but feels insulted by bureaucracy
When he is described on the list
As 'slightly wounded' when at present
He is confined to bed, suffering

From two bullet wounds in each leg
And three on the right arm, not to speak
Of an injury to his left ear from a piece of shell
And the loss of one eye.

The ward is full of Dublin Fusiliers,
Inniskillings and Connaught Rangers.
All light-hearted and full of high spirits,
As all Irish patients usually are.

Private O'Shane from the Fusiliers wants to know
If the Boers grow after the rain like mushrooms…
"There are Irishmen fighting for the Transvaal
Are there not O'Shane?"

"Sure Yes… a few fellows they have come out
Of Ireland. A green flag with a harp in the centre
And gold fringe all around but
(and here O'Shane blushes…)

We can fight with the best of them."
Whereupon there is quite a murmur of assent
Throughout the ward, for upon the Irish Brigades
In the present war, the heaviest blows have fallen.

The extraction of a bullet is no longer
An interesting operation
For bullet wounds are as plentiful
As blackberries on a hedge.'

Unknown Nurse

Unknown nurses –
who look like they know a thing or two

Notes: Part 2
Getting Stuck In

On Patrol

Told to me by Trooper Theodore Fleming of Bethune's Mounted Infantry. Patrols were vital for many reasons, and not just reconnaissance to gather intelligence but to map the land, to see who had passed by, which farms were used as overnight bases in an attempt to keep track of certain commandos. They also had to pass messages, to decoy troops, to leave false trails and of course to engage the enemy. Patrols of four men were really scouts. Larger units were used in pre-planned drives or even pre-planned battles. Ambush was always on the cards.

When the guerrilla war really kicked in mounted infantry were needed more than ever. And the men came from far and wide. Some units like the City Imperial Volunteers were funded by the City of London and the Lord Mayor. Others like the Scottish Horse were funded by aristocrats like Lord Tullibardine or Lord Strathcona who formed Strathcona's Horse. His unit was largely recruited from the North-West Mounted Police who brought with them the Stetson, which became very popular with Baden-Powell who ordered 10,000 of them.

Some units were named after their original Colonels like Colonel Bethune of 16th Lancers who formed Bethune's Mounted Infantry or Rimington's Guides named after Major Mike Rimington who was in the 6th Inniskilling Dragoons and had been to Keble College, Oxford. They were also known as Rimington's Tigers because they wore a band of leopard skin around their slouch hats. Also known as the 'Night Cats' they often worked behind Boer lines in the dark. Every man in Rimington's Corps of Guides not only had to speak English but Afrikaans and a native dialect as well. They were usually armed with carbines and pistols, and often worked ahead of the main army and on the flanks. Later on in the war they were called Damant's Horse.

Other mounted units were named after locations like the Natal Carbineers or the Kimberley Mounted Rifles. The range of volunteer and quasi-military units was enormous. There were hundreds of them. Some were very prestigious like The South African Light Horse which

Rimington's Tigers making themselves at home. Lunch tinned

was largely funded by Wernher, Beit & Co who speculated in gold and diamonds and controlled De Beers. The Boer War fast became a private war, good for business. As with the Imperial Light Horse these units were often recruited from Uitlanders who had left the Rand quickly. Some of these units were very difficult to get into and men had to be very good horsemen and excellent shots to qualify. The work was difficult and dangerous, and the sun gruelling.

For the last 18 months of the war the main occupation of the mounted troops was to sweep the countryside looking for traces of commandos and reporting back. A commando was anything up to 1,000 men or more. The country was divided into large areas with barbed wire and blockhouses which were manned. It was a bit like pheasant shooting with long drives from one group of soldiers towards another. The commandos had the uncanny knack of knowing what was going on and often evaded these sweeps. Only when one or other side was trapped would there be a shoot out. Not very sporting. The Boers naturally enough carried wirecutters, and often cut just enough wire to let their horses through.

Some commandos acted as cavalry and others ended up as mounted infantry. In other words the horse got you to the battle and away again. As the war progressed some Boers switched from the Mauser to the captured British .303 long Lee Enfield as there was far more ammunition available. They also needed biltong, rusk and coffee.

The commando was commanded by a kommandant and each ward by a veldkornet or field cornet like a sergeant. The Boers often fought in family groups under a single corporal. There was a democratic structure and hierarchy, a field cornet was the elected leader of the ward. Some commandos were also drawn from local police units.

There were also international commandos: American, French, German, Dutch, Irish, Italian, Russian, Scandinavian and Swiss which operated rather like the International Brigades during the Spanish Civil War.

Out on patrol things could easily go wrong as happened to a squadron of Bethune's Horse under Captain Goff, which was ambushed at Scheepers Nek, about six miles south-west of Vryheid on 20 May 1900. They lost twenty-seven killed, twenty-five wounded, eleven taken prisoner and twenty-nine horses killed. The guerrilla war was ruthless.

The Battle of Talana

Technically Talana Hill was a British victory but the casualty lists speak for themselves. The British lost 41 men killed, 185 wounded and 220 captured or missing. Most of the captured were from 18th Hussars who had been sent out on reconnaissance. The Boers on the other hand only lost 44 men killed and 66 wounded. The artillery played an important part in the proceedings. The range and fuze settings were vital to get right. Shame about Horn, the Drummer Boy. At the end of the day the Boers very wisely retreated. The British, feeling that they were about to be surrounded abandoned the town and left the wounded there, including General Penn Symons who later died. He had been shot in the stomach.

Lancers

This charge was at the battle of Elandslaagte which was fought on 21 October 1899. Elandslaagte is north-east of Ladysmith on the railway line to Glencoe and Dundee which had small detachment of British troops. The Johannesburg Commando with detachments of German, French, Dutch, American, and Irish volunteers had occupied the railway station and effectively cut off communications. Major General John French was sent out to deal with the matter. The artillery did their thing and the infantry advanced but had some problems with barbed wire. There was a bit of a scuffle and a Boer counter attack led by General Kock dressed in his top hat and Sunday best. He was later killed. Then as the Boers were eventually routed and started leaving the battle field the British secret weapon was unleashed. Four hundred lancers and dragoons. They charged two or three times and hit the Boer column broadside on in the dusk and

Charge of 5th Lancers at Elandslaagte 21 October 1899

killed many of them with their lances and sabres. One of the few times there was a full blooded cavalry charge in the war.

The regiments involved in the cavalry charge were the 5th Irish Lancers and the 5th Dragoons. 'Most excellent pig sticking – a terrible thing but you have to do it.' was how they phrased it.

It may seem savage today but there had been an earlier incident when the Boers had appeared to surrender. They had raised a flag and the infantry emerged from their cover and the cavalry came up from the flank. When they were within forty yards the flag came down and the Boers, including their General Kock resumed firing at close range hitting quite a few. This was not seen as honourable behaviour.

Needless to say 'pig sticking' did not go down well with the Boers. The Johannesburg Commando had effectively been annihilated. They had bitten off more than they could chew.

George Lynch represented the *Illustrated London News* during the Boer War and at one point he was captured by the Boers whilst trying to escape from Ladysmith. This description of Elandslaagte comes from *Impressions of a War Correspondent* published in 1903.

Battle of Modder River
28 November 1899

This was complete disaster for the British even though they technically won the battle. They walked straight into a trap. This was the third battle that week. They had won the two previous battles of Belmont and Graspan by bombarding the kopjes – the hilltops and ridges – and

Argyll & Sutherland Highlanders dash across the Modder River 28 November 1899

then taking them with the bayonet. Tactics that worked in the Peninsular War and Crimea so why not here ? The Boers gave ground and legged it at the last minute on their ponies having inflicted several hundred casualties with only light losses to themselves.

The British were fighting their way up the railway line to relieve Kimberley. The next obstacle was the Modder River and the British assumed that the Boers would try and hold the hills as before. But the Boers played a cunning trick and dug their trenches down by the river bank and camouflaged them with willow and mimosa. Modder River Halt at that point was a small resort for the well-to-do of Kimberley who would often come out for their Sunday lunch, hence the hotels and the availability of gin. Lord Methuen simply marched two brigades across a plain in a night march to reach the river by dawn. It was by all accounts a wonderful morning and the troops ambled up for several miles. Then, when they got close to the river, three thousand Mausers opened up on them and any self respecting soldier who wasn't hit, lay down and stayed there till dusk. They could see nothing at all, and were not able to shoot back very easily with very little cover. The Boers had effectively ambushed two brigades. No mean achievement. Only a few managed to cross the river.

Casualties were very high. It was the first time that Mausers had been used with trenches and the effect was shattering. Some of the worst affected troops were the Guards and the Argyll and Sutherland Highlanders who were wearing kilts and were easily picked off by snipers. They all had the backs of their knees very badly burnt. Water was at a premium. If the Boers had held their fire till they were only 500 yards away the casualties would have been much higher.

The Boer generals who came up with the novel idea of digging trenches were Koos de la Rey and Piet Cronjé. It was the very first modern battle. They had rewritten the rules of war. Technically it was a British victory because the Boers legged it in the night but once again they had inflicted very high casualties. The battle is also known in Afrikaans as *Slag van die Twee Riviere*, the 'Battle of the Two Rivers', because there was also a tributary of the Modder called the Riet which the British were unaware of until the battle itself took place. When they got to the hotel they found lots of empty gin bottles. The trenches were knee deep in cartridge cases. After the battle Lord Rothschild sent Lord Methuen a case of champagne as a token of thanks. The army was slowly edging its way towards the diamond mines at Kimberley

Kilts

With such keen eyed marksmen able to 'pick off' men at over 2,000 yards camouflage was essential and the Boers 'picked off' many officers, not just because they were in front but because they had badges of rank and wore different hats. Some even rode on white horses which was asking for trouble. This loss was especially felt in the Highland regiments where the wearing of kilts,

The Highland Light Infantry on the march
with slouch hats and khaki aprons

cross straps, spats and sporran was a matter of honour, and in Methuen's army there was a whole Highland Brigade. Very quickly they learnt after Modder River and Magersfontein to be as dull as possible to blend into the veld. Even officers carried rifles to make it look as if they were ordinary soldiers. The kilt was marvellous in many ways but alas it offered no protection against the sun on the back of the knees for soldiers lying down. Terrible cases of sunburn were recorded. The problem of camouflage in the Highland regiments was cured when khaki aprons were issued. Some of the Highland Regiments also had Mounted Infantry units.

So desperate was the need for camouflage that Fox Brothers of Wellington in Somerset developed a new serge drape which they called khaki. At the height of the Boer War they produced 30,000 yards of khaki a week.

Battle of Magersfontein

After the battle of Modder River the Boers had withdrawn a few miles up the railway line and were believed to be dug in around Spyfontein and Magersfontein. The artillery pounded the hill tops and made the same mistake as they had down at Modder River. The Boers were nowhere to be seen. The battle took place on 11 December 1899 which gave the Boers plenty of time to dig trenches at night and Lord Methuen made exactly the same mistake. Only this time he sent the whole of the Highland Brigade into the trap. These were the 2nd Black Watch, 2nd Seaforth Highlanders, 1st Argyll & Sutherland Highlanders and the Highland Light Infantry. It was a night march and they were led by Major General Andrew Wauchope. A lean Scot who had fought in the Ashanti Wars, Egypt and Sudan and had fought at the Battle of Omdurman. He knew what he was doing and had very grave

Major-General Andrew Wauchope

misgivings about this night march, once more across a flat plain into an area that had barely been reconnoitred and might be heavily defended. His canny instinct was that this method of attack was not a good idea at all.

To make matters worse it started raining. Their navigation was spot on and just as they were about to change from marching in quarter column into 'open order' they were spotted by the Boers, when they were only 400 yards from the trenches. These trenches were well camouflaged by willow and mimosa at the bottom of the hill. Yet again thousands of Mausers opened up. There was great confusion but there was a charge: some fled while others lay down. To make matters worse there was barbed wire and when they

Magersfontein - Boer trench Shades of 1914

The Seaforth Highlanders in full ceremonial rig

charged the trenches they got their kilts stuck on the wire. Shades of things to come in the First War. As at Modder River the men that were not hit were forced to lie down all day and suffer the bullets and the sun and a bitter thirst. This time the Boers stood their ground even though the small Scandinavian Commando was completely wiped out.

It was a total disaster which made the Battle of Modder River ten days before seem like a picnic. Over 700 in the Highland Brigade were killed or wounded in the first five minutes it is said. The 2nd Black Watch bore the brunt of this and lost over 300 men. Andrew Wauchope was one of the first casualties. News of the battle was very slow to filter back home as censorship was in place. Reports in the newspapers did not really surface until January 1900.

What was left of the Highland Brigade was stunned and shocked. What is fascinating is that one of the soldiers wrote a ballad that was turned into a poem which recorded the events of that day. This was eventually printed in the *Morning Leader* on 10 February 1900 and other newspapers. There are several versions of the poem which differ on certain points. In places it is highly critical of the senior officers and their planning. It feels almost as if it was written in the middle of the First World War and its sentiments are echoed in Siegfried Sassoon's jocular style.

The refrain 'Tommy Atkins' is very like Kipling and maybe it is no coincidence that Rudyard Kipling was in Cape Town in January and February 1900. He went up to Bloemfontein to work briefly on a newspaper called *The Friend* with the war correspondents Leo Amery, H.A. Gwynne, Perceval Landon and Julian Ralph.

'All that was left of them' – The Black Watch after the Battle of Magersfontein, from a drawing by R Caton Woodville.

The real author of 'The Battle of Magersfontein' is however still a mystery. One version is held at the Cape Town Archives Repository (Acc 411) and another in The Strange Africana Collection Johannesburg (S Pam 821 BLA). Copies are also held in the Black Watch Museum in Perth. Some say the soldier was wounded and his words were taken down at De Aar in a convalescent camp a few days later. His name is occasionally given as Private Smith but there were at least five Private Smiths in the 2nd Black Watch. Two were killed and three wounded at Magersfontein. Take your pick. A later version is credited to Corporal David McMahon.

Barbed Wire Debate

There was much debate in military circles about the barbed wire at the Battle of Magersfontein. Some soldiers of the Highland Brigade encountered it, others did not. One diagonal line was probably the border between the Orange Free State and Cape Colony that ran across the battle field. Some wire was barbed, some was not. Other accounts say that there were two lines of barbed wire in front of the Boer trenches, none higher than knee level. Also there was old agricultural barbed wire fencing from Magersfontein farm which is the wire mentioned by Michael Davitt in his book *Boer Fight for Freedom.*

Davitt (1846–1906) was an outspoken Irish M.P. who had founded The Irish National Land League. He

More barbed wire – this time at Heidelberg

resigned from the House of Commons on 26 October 1899 in protest at the Boer War and went to observe things from the Boer lines. Though he started out as a Fenian and was sentenced to fifteen years hard labour in Dartmoor Prison (he served half his sentence) his subsequent non-violent movement was an inspiration to among others the crofters of Scotland and Mahatma Gandhi. There were strong connections between the Irish and the Boers and there was an Irish Commando in the Transvaal under John MacBride which had about 500 members, mostly from the gold mines.

The extract from Arthur Conan Doyle comes from his great tome *The Great Boer War* which runs to thirty-nine chapters. Originally brought out in 1900 it ran to sixteen editions by 1902. As he says 'This book was begun in England and continued on board a steamer, but the greater part was written in a hospital tent in the intervals during the epidemic at Bloemfontein.' The epidemic was enteric fever (typhoid). Conan Doyle worked as a doctor at the Langman Field Hospital.

The use of barbed wire was seen as a fiendish device, and this was the first battle where its use in defence was proven beyond all measure. As to the extent of the barbed wire, Richard McKenzie the archivist at The Black Watch Museum, very kindly looked at interviews with survivors which they hold and says that 'Men of A and B Company, Black Watch, encountered the wire and were disrupted by it. But the men of E Company encountered no wire and were free to charge at the Boer lines.'

One of the war correspondents for the *Daily News* said of the troops that: 'the wires caught them round the legs till they floundered like trapped wolves'. Warfare was now very clearly entering a new and terrible phase. Photographs show the sort of wire defences that were constructed.

Death from a Mauser Bullet

This description of one casualty from the Devon Regiment at the Battle of Elandslaagte comes from *Impressions of a War Correspondent* by George Lynch published in 1903. George Lynch was a *Daily Express* war correspondent and also wrote for the *Illustrated London News*. One feels that he wrote the piece to spare the gory details from anxious relatives back in England.

What he is trying to describe is that death from a Mauser bullet is quick and humane. Just depends where you are hit. The overall casualties for Elandslaagte were only fifty-five dead and 205 wounded.

Like many war correspondents George Lynch thought the Boer War was over in June 1900 when the British army entered Pretoria, and so he sailed on to the next war in China, The Boxer Rebellion, little realising that the Boer War which was now entering its guerrilla phase, still had nearly two years to run.

Dum-Dum

Captain Neville Sneyd Bertie-Clay really did exist. He seems like a character from one of John Betjeman's poems and would no doubt have played a mean game of tennis with Miss Joan Hunter Dunn.

The dum-dum bullet, however, was a real bone of contention. The Mark IV was first used at the Battle of Omdurman in 1898. That year the German government lodged a protest against their use, claiming that the wounds produced by the Mark IV were excessive and inhumane, thus violating the laws of war. The Hague Convention in 1899 outlawed them on a vote 22-2. The treaty was signed on 29 July 1899 but did not come into force until 4 September 1900, which may indicate that their early use in the opening battles of the Boer War was not technically illegal but was certainly ill advised and very bad publicity. The wounds caused by dum-dum bullets when they expanded were horrific. Hunters used the technique by cutting a cross in the nose of the old lead bullets. Neither Britain nor the Boer Republics had in fact signed the convention.

The British however had already issued vast stocks of them to their troops in India so they naturally enough brought them with them when they came over in their troopships from Bombay and Calcutta. In 1899 Britain had a stock of 172 million expanding bullets, of which 66 million had been delivered to British bases worldwide.

The Hague Convention of 1899 was fascinating because it not only outlawed dum-dum bullets but it outlawed a) Discharge of Projectiles and Explosives from Balloons or by Other New Analogous Methods (i.e. aircraft) and b) the Use of Projectiles with the Sole Object to Spread Asphyxiating Poisonous Gases. Both of which problems reared their ugly heads during the First World War.

Both sides used dum-dum bullets but one suspects that most of the ones used by the Boers were captured from the British at Dundee after Elandslaagte and Talana and would only fit captured Lee Enfield rifles.

Both sides were well aware of their illegality and having them on one's person could mean summary execution, so Winston Churchill was let off very lightly indeed. It seems that war correspondents often had to fight for their lives. The Boers treated Winston as a prisoner of war and regarded him as 'very dangerous indeed'.

The war correspondent who lost his arm to a dum-dum bullet at the Battle of Belmont was Edward Frederick Knight. He was also a barrister and travel writer. He had seen the Franco-Prussian War of 1870, the Russian-Turkish War of 1877-78, as well as the wars in the Sudan. He had also been in Hunza, Gilgit and Ladakh and wrote a book called *Where Three Empires Meet*. He was a war correspondent for *The Times* and even after he lost his arm, he covered the Russo-

Funeral at Estcourt November 1899

Japanese War of 1904-5 where he was reported as having been killed. The *New York Times* ran his obituary, but he was alive and well and went on to live for another twenty years. *The Morning Post* was unlucky for they not only lost the services of E.F. Knight on 23 November 1899 but their other roving war correspondent in Natal, Winston Churchill, who had been captured eight days earlier on 15 November 1899. It all made good copy and the newspapers were much in demand back home. Indeed one could say that they drove the war. Being captured made Churchill's name and even helped his career when he later entered Parliament.

R.I.P.

Truce at Magersfontein

The slaughter was so appalling at the Battle of Magersfontein that many of the dead and wounded were lying well within earshot of the Boer lines. So General Cronjé himself, unarmed, stood up, waved his arms and sent a message to Lord Methuen suggesting that he brought some ambulances across, which he did. One officer commented – 'Quite decent fellows the Boers'. When the horse drawn ambulances had retired the battle commenced. The report was only published on 8 January 1900 so it had been held up for nearly a month.

The *London Standard* journalist has yet to be identified. This report is mentioned by Michael Davitt in his book *Boer Fight for Freedom* (1904)

There was another *London Standard* war correspondent, William Maxwell but he was by then bottled up in Ladysmith. He survived enteric fever and later reported on the Siege of Ladysmith. Another famous war reporter in Ladysmith, George Harrington Steevens, did not survive enteric fever and died six weeks before the town was relieved. He worked for the *Daily Mail* and regularly contributed to the *Ladysmith Lyre*. His book *From Capetown to Ladysmith* was published posthumously. Being a war correspondent was indeed a dangerous business.

Interestingly in 1915, William Maxwell was the press officer for Sir Ian Hamilton during the Gallipoli campaign and was effectively the press censor on yet another military disaster, i.e. he was employed to suppress news rather than report it accurately. For this he was knighted in 1919.

Burial place of Highlanders who fell at Magersfontein

Burial Parties

Michael Davitt's gruesome quote comes from his book *Boer Fight for Freedom*. With so many dead it must have been horrendous and it was midsummer. Some of these war time quotes have to be taken with a large pinch of salt: Davitt was no lover of the British and the British Army but it has the awful, sordid ring of truth to it.

The short quote from the Colour Sergeant comes from *South Africa and the Transvaal War* by Louis Creswicke and published in 1900.

When the Balloon Goes Up

War balloons were first used in the Boer War by Royal Engineers at Magersfontein and in the Siege of Ladysmith. At the beginning of the war they had twenty balloons. They were khaki in colour and filled with hydrogen. They had a wicker basket, could carry two men and could rise to about 4,000 ft. They were inflated and then were towed around by bullock carts, and could stay inflated for up to twenty days.

No. 1 Section under Captain H.B. Jones arrived in Cape Town on 22 November with three officers, thirty-four NCOs and other ranks, three wagons, eleven balloons as well as special equipment for the generation and storage of hydrogen. The balloons were rushed up to the front and arrived with Lord Methuen on the day of the Battle of Magersfontein. If Lord Methuen had waited one day longer it is just possible they would have spotted the

Getting a war balloon ready. Testing the telegraphic apparatus

Boer trenches in advance which might have altered the plan of attack. As it was the balloon went up on the day of the battle and did in fact report certain Boer troop movements of reserves being brought into the line. With excellent telescopes they could see the action quite

War balloon ready for take off

clearly. Also they had a direct telephone link with the ground straight to the general's headquarters. They were also able to make sketches and maps a bit like the early eighteenth century drawings of Kip and Knyff.

Balloons were also used in the Siege of Ladysmith and were very useful for spotting enemy movements and for taking the first aerial photographs.

The balloons were made out of small sections of cattle intestines called in the trade 'gold beater's skin'. It was light, strong and flexible. The skill came in stitching the small sections together and repairing them in the field. They made their own hydrogen. Balloons sometimes worked in pairs to get more accurate surveys. Only one or two were ever shot down as they worked out of range of even the Mausers. Once or twice they had to retreat in a hurry towing the balloon behind them.

Banjo Patterson, the famous Australian Bush poet and *Sydney Morning Herald* war correspondent mentioned a balloon going up on 23 February 1900 just before the attack on Paardeberg. 'The war balloon has just gone by on a cart swaying in the wind, and as soon as its report comes in we may see another attack on (General) Cronjé.'

So the expression 'When the Balloon Goes Up' derives from the Boer War and not the First War as many suppose. Observation balloons had first been used during the French Revolutionary Wars at the Battle of Fleurus in 1794. They were also used in the American Civil War.

Conan Doyle on Colenso

Colenso was a major battle on the Tugela River. It was a railway station on the line from Ladysmith and just up from Chieveley which is where young Winston got caught. Unlike the previous battles which were to aid the relief of Kimberley, these battles were to relieve Ladysmith. Yet again the Boers dug in on the river banks and had them fooled. It was fought on 15 December 1899 only four days after the debacle at Magersfontein. There had also been a third battle which didn't go too well – Stormberg with nearly 100 casualties and almost 700 captured. It was dubbed Black Week.

At Colenso 4,500 Boers defeated an army of 14,000 and inflicted very heavy casualties. Buller's army lost 143 killed, 756 wounded and 220 captured. Boer casualties were eight killed and thirty wounded. The Boers once more knew exactly what they were doing and they didn't have balloons. What Conan Doyle is describing is the advance of the Irish Brigade which consisted of the Royal Inniskilling Fusiliers, the Connaught Rangers, the Dublin Fusiliers, and the Border Regiment.

Predictably many men were lost to accurate Mauser fire, the field guns got a hammering as well and had to be saved. Even so ten guns had to be abandoned. Lord Robert's son, Freddy was killed here, though he did win a Victoria Cross. Little consolation to his father. Black Week was really black and the Boers had every right to be pleased with themselves. Yet again the farmers had stopped the whole British Army in its tracks.

Mahatma Gandhi at Spion Kop

The battle of Spion Kop (Spioenkop) was yet another unmitigated disaster. The battle took place not far from Colenso 23–24 January 1900. The Boers could see them coming from a mile off. Spion Kop was a large long hill with two summits. The British troops climbed up in a night attack in thick mist and surprised a small party of Boers whom they displaced at the point of the bayonet. So far so good. They then tried to dig in, but they only had twenty picks and twenty shovels. Not enough for 1,000 men and anyway the ground was mostly rock. When dawn broke they found that they were on the lower of the two summits and they were overlooked by a large body of Boers who were itching to have go at them. Louis Botha was in command. The Boers even charged to take the ridge line and there was hand to hand fighting. A stalemate then ensued and artillery on both sides began to have a go. The battle swayed backwards and forwards.

Many infantry men were killed where they lay in their trenches which were very shallow.

There was no water and the wounded suffered from heatstroke. Winston Churchill was also there, having escaped from a school in Pretoria and was now Lieutenant in the South African Light Horse. He was employed as a courier and saw the battle field for himself and was appalled at the casualties and the nature of the wounds. In the end there were 1,500 British casualties. The British retreated. The Boers held the hill but they had some 330 casualties, which demoralised them no end. It was a very hard fight indeed.

As far as the wounded were concerned they were mostly looked after and retrieved from the battle field by a variety of medical teams. One of which was the Natal Indian Ambulance Corps nominally under the Red Cross. It was led by a feisty Indian lawyer called Mohandas K. Gandhi. They numbered about 300 volunteer Indians and about 800 indentured labourers. They were supported and trained in first aid work by Dr Lancelot Parker Booth who had founded St Aidan's Mission in Durban.

As Gandhi said 'When the war was declared, my personal sympathies were all with the Boers, but I believed then that I had yet no right, in such cases, to enforce my individual convictions.'

He goes on 'Suffice it to say that my loyalty to the British rule drove me to participation with the British in that war. I felt that, if I demanded rights as a British citizen, it was also my duty, as such, to participate in the defence of the British Empire. I held then that India could achieve her complete emancipation only within and through the British Empire. So I collected together as many comrades as possible, and with very great difficulty got their services accepted as an ambulance corps.'

The Indians were not trained for combat and yet at Spion Kop they were asked to work under fire, which they agreed to. Their job was to get the wounded back to

Indian stretcher bearers under fire

the base hospital at Frere which was over 20 miles away, no easy matter. Their bravery and hard work won the admiration of the British soldiers and broke down many of the traditional class barriers.

As Gandhi says again: 'The relations formed with the whites during the war were of the sweetest. We had come in contact with thousands of Tommies. They were friendly with us and thankful for being there to serve them.'

It even went one step further when they were carrying the body of Lord Robert's son back to Chieveley.

'It was a sultry day – the day of our march. Everyone was thirsting for water. There was a tiny brook on the way where we could slake our thirst. But who was to drink first? We had proposed to come in after the Tommies had finished. But they would not begin first and urged us to do so, and for a while a pleasant competition went on for giving precedence to one another.'

General Roberts under the watchful eye of his Indian bodyguard - Pretoria 1900

Although civilians, the Indian bearers were paid a daily allowance from the Department of Public Works and they did receive medals, however they were not considered eligible to receive the Queen's Chocolate, which seemed a bit unfair. More than 10,000 Indians were sent to work during the Boer War and over 1,000 were inside Ladysmith when it was besieged. No one knows how many died.

Vere Stent, a Reuters correspondent described the work of the Indian Ambulance Corps in the *Illustrated Star* of Johannesburg, July 1911. Vere Stent was owner and editor of the *Pretoria News 1903-1920*. He also worked as a war correspondent in the First War.

It is a wonderful and enduring image to have seen M.K. Gandhi himself on the roadside chewing on a British army biscuit. No doubt he was also secretly chewing over his ideas on Independence for India.

Slightly Wounded

This is an interesting piece which is only a small extract from a much longer piece which eventually ended up in the *Otago Times* in New Zealand. It is also a morale boosting piece destined for the newspapers in the run up to Christmas and making light of the disasters. It is an anonymous piece so it is very difficult to say who the writer was, but one possible name at least has emerged. That of Agnes McCready, a locally employed nurse at Fort Napier Hospital, Pietermaritzburg. She was on the spot and in the early days they needed every nurse they could lay their hands on. It so happens that she was also a correspondent for some Australian newspapers and her news would have been syndicated in Sydney to New Zealand which is why it found its way to the *Otago Times*. She later worked at No. 7 General Hospital Pretoria and the convent hospital Estcourt.

This piece can be dated fairly precisely because at one point it mentions news of General Gatacre's 'reverse at Stormberg' on 10 December 1899 but it also mentions Colenso which was on 15 December at the end of Black Week. So this must have been written around 18 December 1899. At Stormberg, an important rail junction, a small incompetently led British force was hammered very hard by the Boers. The British did yet another night march with fixed bayonets and walked into an ambush. Twenty killed, sixty-eight wounded, 696 were left behind by mistake and captured. No doubt Private Brown of the Northumberland Fusiliers was wounded here. There is mention of a shell from Colenso in a shop window and all three of the Irish regiments mentioned, fought there and had heavy casualties.

What is fascinating is the discussion about the Irish Brigades. The Irish Transvaal Brigade (also known as MacBride's Brigade) was mostly made up of Irish miners who happened to be in the Transvaal and supported the Boer cause. They operated from September 1899 to September 1900. The brigade fought in about twenty engagements, with eighteen men killed and about seventy wounded from a complement of no more than about 500 men. At the Siege of Ladysmith, they serviced the famous Boer artillery piece, called Long Tom, and they fought at the Battle of Colenso 15 December 1899, which would explain why one group of determined Irishmen were fighting another group of determined Irishmen. Shades of 1916 and auguries of things to come let alone the bitter civil war in 1922.

Having worked in the gold mines, the pro-Boer Irish miners were also demolition experts and delayed the British advance to Pretoria by blowing up bridges.

Nurses were employed by at least three organisations, apart from the Red Cross: Princess Christian's Army Nursing Reserve, the Army Nursing Service and the Natal Volunteer Medical Corps. Princess Christian was the third daughter of Queen Victoria. Army nurses were paid by the War Office at the rate of £40 a year from the time they entered service in South Africa. Conditions in the tented hospitals and camps were harsh and forty-seven nurses are known to have died of disease.

Dead bodies after the battle of Spion Kop 24 January 1900

Part 3

Besieged

R.S.V.P.

My father was marvellous with horses.
Went off to Ireland to learn the brewing business
From the Guinness family,

And while he was there the Boer War
Broke out. And of course off he went
And joined the army didn't he!

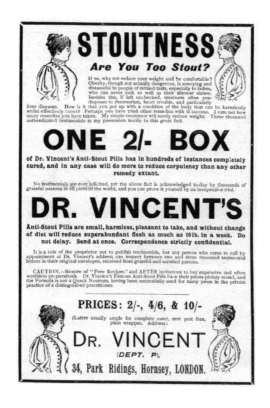

He did send home,
A postcard to 'My sweetheart',
Three leaves from a tree on Table Mountain,

I have them here
And a photograph
Of the Battle of Ladysmith.

He was there in Cape Town
When Churchill was there,
In the same lot.

But it was the siege that he was in
One man in the regiment
Went white overnight with fright.

'Last Gentleman's War ever fought'
He said, though a clergyman
Didn't agree with him.

But then again my father
Hadn't seen the camps –
The women and children herded together.

Kathleen Bennett talking about her father
Private Harry Howlett 18th Hussars

Forced March – Retreat from Dundee

At 4 p.m. a huge water spout was seen
Coming straight for us –
Luckily it broke two miles off.

It would have stampeded every horse in the camp.

The rain then came down
For about three hours in torrents.
Wetting everyone to the skin.

I got my flask filled with whiskey
Neat from Turner of the Sappers
And we kept warm on that.

At about 8 o'clock were given some grub
(Bully beef and bully biscuits
Had been our fare since Friday)
And got six hours sleep.

Since 3 a.m. on Friday until 9 p.m. on Tuesday
I had had none. We moved at 4 a.m.
The most awful night I ever hope to spend.

I kept touch between my section
And that in front of me,
By fastening a white handkerchief over my back.

They could just see this two yards behind me and no more.
The next day we marched into Ladysmith.

Lt Max Chevenix Trench R.A.
Sunday 22 October – Thursday 26 Oct 1899

2nd Devons entering Ladysmith March 1900

Siege of Ladysmith
10 February 1900

Dear Kathleen,
101 not out, Ladysmith still batting
On an uneven wicket

And on Christmas Day
They sent over a plum pudding
Inside a shell wrapped in a Union Jack

Which did not explode.
'Compliments of the season.'
Quite a sense of humour. The Boers

Then we had to start killing
The cavalry horses,
Just a steak once a day, no vegetables.

*Signalling to Ladysmith with Naval searchlight at Frere – by bouncing
morse code messages off the undersides of the clouds.*

Better than tough T.O. old trek ox.
So it was a pound of horsemeat
Half a pound of biscuits or mealie bread

One ounce of sugar and one sixteenth
Of an ounce of tea. Still they shelled us
Long Tom, enteric and dysentery

Not sure which was worst
Lady Smith herself would have
Stuck it out with panache.
George White stayed behind, dithered a bit
Powerful too, the sailors I mean
And barefoot. Terrible goings on.

Lady Anne and Princess Victoria.
Keep up quite a dialogue with Long Tom
Puffing Billy and Silent Susan.

And then damn it all on New Year's Day
One officer was killed during a cricket match
Bowling he was. Very unsporting.

Needless to say the match went on
Not sure when I will be coming home
We hear artillery further to the south.
Poor old Buller trying his best
To break through I believe.
Very hot indeed. But no real news.

Except occasionally by heliograph winking
Or searchlight at night - morse code
Bounced off the clouds –
An armoured train further down the line
Manned by sailors. *Terrible* I believe.
Even then the Boers try to interrupt it.

There were a few racing pigeons
But they have long since gone
Would have tasted rather good.
Chevril not bad at all
Rations in the hospital cut again
Very strange feeling without the horses.

No doubt we shall chew the harness.
Very bored, very tired, very thin
Yours ever – Harry.

Long Tom not so long – with barrel blown off.

Boredom

The main problem facing the garrison
And civilian population
Before disease began to take its toll
Was boredom.

White recognised this clearly enough
When he told his staff:
'Gentlemen we have two things to do –
To kill time and to kill Boers –
Both equally difficult.'

To begin with there was plenty going on
To keep people occupied despite the shelling.

The women of Ladysmith gave tennis parties
And there were gymkhanas.
Cricket, football and polo
(while the ponies were still strong enough)
Were all played.

A military tournament was arranged
By a committee of senior soldiers
Under Hunter's chairmanship.

On the river there were races in tubs
And bathing parties were organised.

Once however, complaints were made
To the Town Council that soldiers
Were bathing naked in the river
And that this must be forbidden
Because the ladies
Enjoyed walking on its banks.

On Sundays there were always church parades,
And very important there was no shelling
On the day of rest, at least to begin with.

Archie Hunter

General Sir Archibald Hunter

Alarms

Life in Ladysmith was a little worse than being
confined in a jail, for a jail has at least the advantage
of being a comparatively safe and secluded habitation.

The smoke of 'Long Tom' on Bulwana, which was the gun
of the greatest terror to the inhabitants could be seen
for twenty-five seconds before the shell struck in the town,

and, in order to warn people of its coming,
sentinels were constantly on watch
to look for the smoke and give the alarm.

Cronjé with his 'Big Gun' (Long Tom) at the Siege of Mafeking.
Piet Cronjé is the man holding the whip.

At one hotel the signal was the ringing of a bell;
the Indian coolies used an iron bar swung from a rope
which they beat with another iron bar,

and the different regiments enjoyed the services of their buglers.
So that the instant a white puff of smoke
and a hot flash of fire appeared on Bulwana,

there would be a thrilling toot on the bugles,
a chorus of gongs, bells, and tin pans,
and the sound of many scampering footsteps.

It was like a village of prairie dogs diving
into their underground homes.
But the familiarity soon bred indifference,

and after a few weeks only a small number of the people
sought refuge under the iron roofs
and sand-bags but walked the streets

as freely as though the shells weighing
a hundred pounds were as innocent of harm
as the dropping of the gentle dew from heaven.

Richard Harding Davis

Tied Piper

Every morning during the siege
He played the pipes, some tunes chosen no doubt
To evoke the feeling of longing for home
And the tartan shore, the mountains

That some might not ever see again.
Drones of a different kind,
Double reeds and semi quavers
Pibroch and chanter at his elbow.

How they would have longed
For a highland glen or the chance
To tickle trout in a stream
Or gaze upon the glassy mirror of a long loch.

No doubt when the diet was scant,
These images kept them fed.
Thin air and oats, the salty water,
Ladysmith had its own way

Of making itself felt beneath the belt.
Besieged by music
Undaunted by the shells,
The highlander survived.

Later on I was shown his pipes
They lay in pride of place
Upon a chest of drawers
At the top of the stairs, slightly dusty

And had been played by his son,
Who was at another siege,
In another war, and at his own funeral,
There was of course, a piper.

The father of Kenneth Cameron

Boer marksmen

Malaria

'My father, he had malaria very badly
During the South African War
And I can remember
When I was in my teens
He had recurring bouts

And he would be shaking and shaking
Till the whole bed shook
But eventually it seemed to die away.
But it affected one of his eyes
And he was eventually blind in that eye.'

As if Anopholes was conducting
Her own guerrilla warfare behind the scenes,
Getting under the skin of the military,
Biting back, drawing you down
Into the world of fever.

Hot and then cold, then stiff
The body trapped on the rack.
No way out. The evening meal
An ambush, years later when you least
Expect it. Not so useless after all.

**Based on Kathleen Bennett talking about her father,
Harry Howlett 18th Hussars**

Scurvy

The men are getting very weak
On the low feeding they are getting now.
One or two cases of scurvy.

For the last fortnight or so
We have been eating horses and a few mules.
The worst thing is the low bread ration.

On alternate days we get half pound hard biscuits
Or else quarter pound bread (one big slice)
And four ounces of mealie meal.

My section of chestnuts have suffered very severely.
Nine or ten gun horses and about the whole
Of the ammunition wagon teams have died.

20 February 1900 Ladysmith Lt Max Chevenix Trench R.A.

Concentrated beef and cocoa paste.

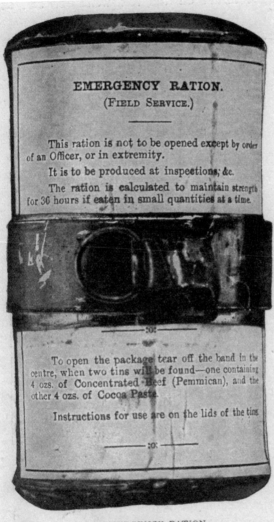

EMERGENCY RATION.

(FIELD SERVICE.)

This ration is not to be opened except by order of an Officer, or in extremity.

It is to be produced at inspections, &c.

The ration is calculated to maintain strength for 36 hours if eaten in small quantities at a time.

To open the package tear off the band in the centre, when two tins will be found—one containing 4 ozs. of Concentrated Beef (Pemmican), and the other 4 ozs. of Cocoa Paste.

Instructions for use are on the lids of the tins.

THE EMERGENCY RATION

Carried by every soldier in his haversack and produced at every inspection. It was the only food available for the men in exposed positions at Magersfontein.

Cigars

When confronted by two horsemen I was asked
if I was an outsider. I was forced to admit that I was.
I felt that I had taken an unwarrantable
Liberty in intruding on a besieged garrison.

I wanted to say that I had lost my way
and had ridden into the town
by mistake, and that I begged
to be allowed to withdraw with apologies.

The other officer woke up suddenly
and handed me a printed list of the prices
which had been paid during the siege
for food and tobacco. He seemed to offer it

as being in some way an official apology
for his starved appearance. The price of cigars
struck me as especially pathetic,
and I commented on it.

The first officer gazed mournfully
at the blazing sunshine before him.
'I have not smoked a cigar in two months', he said.
My surging sympathy, and my terror at again

offending the haughty garrison,
combated so fiercely that it was only
with a great effort that I produced a handful.

'Will you have these?' The other officer
started in his saddle so violently
that I thought his horse had stumbled,
but he also kept his eyes straight in front.
'Thank you, I will take one if I may -

Just one', said the first officer.
'Are you sure I am not robbing you?'
They each took one, but they refused
to put the rest of the cigars in their pockets.

As the printed list stated
that a dozen matches sold for 13/6d
I handed them a box of matches.
Then a beautiful thing happened.

They lit the cigars and at the first taste of the smoke –
and they were not good cigars –
an almost human expression of peace
and good-will and utter abandonment to joy

spread over their yellow skins
and cracked lips and fever-lit eyes.
The first man dropped his reins
and put his hands on his hips

and threw back his head and shoulders
and closed his eyelids.
I felt that I had intruded at a moment
which should have been left sacred.

Richard Harding Davis

Food Auction Prices
SIEGE OF LADYSMITH

I certify that the following are the correct and highest prices realised at my sales by Public Auction during the above Siege,
Joe Dyson, Auctioneer Ladysmith, February 21st, 1900.

	£	s.	d.
14 lbs. Oatmeal	2	19	6
Condensed Milk, per tin	0	10	0
1 lb. Beef Fat	0	11	0
1 lb. Tin Coffee	0	17	0
2 lb. Tin Tongue	1	6	0
1 Sucking Pig	1	17	0
Eggs, per dozen	2	8	0
Fowls, each	0	18	6
4 Small Cucumbers	0	15	6
Green Mealies, each	0	3	8
Small plate Grapes	1	5	0
1 Small plate Apples	0	12	6
1 Plate Tomatoes	0	18	0
1 Vegetable Marrow	1	8	0
1 Plate Eschalots	0	11	0
1 Plate Potatoes	0	19	0
3 Small bunches Carrots	0	9	0
1 Glass Jelly	0	18	0
1 lb. Bottle Jam	1	11	0
1 lb. Tin Marmalade	1	1	0
1 dozen Matches	0	13	6
1 pkt. Cigarettes	1	5	0
50 Cigars	9	5	0
¼ lb. Cake 'Fair Maid' Tobacco	2	5	0
½ lb. Cake 'Fair Maid' Tobacco	3	5	0
1 lb. Sailors Tobacco	2	3	0
¼ lb. tin "Capstan" Navy Cut Tobacco	3	0	0

Relief at Last

It was a pitiful contrast
which the two forces presented.

The men of the garrison were in clean khaki,
pipe-clayed and brushed and polished,
but their tunics hung on them as loosely
as the flag around its pole,
the skin on their cheek-bones
was as tight and as yellow as the belly of a drum,
their teeth protruded through parched,
cracked lips, and hunger, fever,
and suffering stared from out their eyes.

They were so ill and so feeble
that the mere exercise of standing
was too severe for their endurance,
and many of them collapsed,
falling back to the sidewalk,
rising to salute only the first troop
of each succeeding regiment.

This done, they would again sink back
and each would sit leaning
his head against his musket,
or with his forehead resting
heavily on his folded arms.

In comparison the relieving column
looked like giants as they came in
with a swinging swagger,
their uniforms blackened with mud
and sweat and bloodstains,
their faces brilliantly crimsoned
and blistered and tanned by the dust and sun.

They made a picture of strength
and health and aggressiveness.

Richard Harding Davis

"Hello Hubert. How the Devil are you?"
Sir George White welcomes Major Hubert Gough who has just ridden
in for tea. Relief of Ladysmith. 28 Feb 1900

The Devons

Perhaps the contrast was strongest
when the battalion of the Devons
that had been on foreign service
passed the 'reserve' battalion
which had come from England.

The men of the two battalions had parted
five years before in India, and they met again in Ladysmith,
with the men of one battalion lining the streets,
sick, hungry, and yellow,
and the others, who had been fighting
six weeks to reach it, marching toward them,
robust, red-faced, and cheering mightily.

As they met they gave a shout of recognition,
and the men broke ranks and ran forward,
calling each other by name,
embracing, shaking hands,
and punching each other
in the back and shoulders.

It was a sight that very few men watched
unmoved. Indeed, the whole three hours
was one of the most brutal assaults
upon the feelings that it has been my lot to endure.
Brave men saluting brave men.

Richard Harding Davis

Notes: Part 3
Besieged

R.S.V.P.

This is taken from an interview with a lady in my village called Kathleen Bennett, whose father Harry Howlett had been in the Boer War in the 18th Hussars. Family stories about the Boer War are very important as they often cover incidents and events that are glossed over in official histories. Many soldiers in the Boer War then went on to serve in the First War. Harry Howlett stayed in the army, became a sergeant and was awarded a D.C.M. for gallantry at Messines near Ypres in 1914 where he led a charge to retake some ground and saved an officer's life. He later joined the Royal Flying Corps.

Naval 4.7" gun from HMS Terrible *in action at Magersfontein. on home made gun carriage designed by Captain Percy Scott R.N. They required 32 oxen to haul them around.*

Forced March – Retreat from Dundee

The next evening after the Battle of Talana the British decided to retreat and returned to Ladysmith, a long forced march of sixty-four miles over very rough terrain. Very demoralising for all concerned. A journey they accomplished in four very long days and often at night. It was foul weather and the march was very taxing for man and beast. Many supplies and vast quantities of food and ammunition had to be left behind in Dundee.

Siege of Ladysmith

Sieges were an integral part of the early campaign as the Boers had deliberately laid siege to three towns: Kimberley, Mafeking and Ladysmith. In fact Ladysmith was something of a disaster as about 13,000 troops were bottled up there, particularly the cavalry: the 5th Dragoon Guards, 18th and 19th Hussars as well as several other mounted units like the Natal Carbineers. Horses eat oats. Some horses, particularly the grays, had to be dyed khaki so the snipers didn't get them first.

Ladysmith was besieged from 30 October 1899 till 28 February 1900. A total of 118 days. The other two towns besieged during the Boer War were Mafeking with Colonel Baden-Powell at the helm, who had learnt a lot about scouting from the Zulus and held out for 217 days; and Kimberley under Colonel Robert Kekewich who had fought in Burma and Sudan. Kimberley held out for 124 days.

Ladysmith was named in 1850 after a fine looking aristocratic Spanish lady who was the wife of Sir Harry Smith who was Governor of The Cape Colony. Her real name was Juana María de los Dolores de León Smith or

Map of Natal showing Ladysmith, Colenso, Spion Kop etc

Lady Smith for short. She had herself been besieged during the Peninsular War in the fortress of Badajoz in 1812 and at the end of the siege, when the real horrors unfolded, she with her sister, sought protection, and befriended a few British Army officers one of whom, Brevet Major Harry Smith proposed to her on the spot. She was only fourteen but accompanied him on all his future campaigns. She was very brave, well liked by the Duke of Wellington and adored by the troops. When her husband was knighted she became a Lady, which in effect she already was. She died in 1872.

Ladysmith the town was defended by General Sir George White, a brave Irishman who had served in the Gordon Highlanders and had won a Victoria Cross during the Second Afghan War. Interestingly his son also entered the army won a D.S.O. in the Boer War then turned tail and became an founder member of the Irish Citizens Army and was close friends with James Connolly. He later served in the Spanish Civil War as a communist. One wonders what his father would have thought.

At sixty-four, Sir George White was however a bit past his sell by date, and the command structure was kept together by two stalwarts: Colonel Ian Hamilton who had been wounded in the wrist at Majuba Hill and would later be in charge of the disastrous Gallipoli campaign and Colonel Archibald Hunter who had been on the expedition in Sudan to try and rescue General Gordon. Also in Ladysmith was Colonel Henry Rawlinson who, after the end of the First World War, was sent to Archangel in Northern Russia to supervise the evacuation of the British anti-Bolshevik forces based there.

Two other officers who distinguished themselves under Kitchener were Major General French and his Chief of Staff, Major Douglas Haig who both escaped on the last train to leave Ladysmith, which was riddled with bullets. Both later became important figures and household names in the First War.

The Boer War and the Siege of Ladysmith honed down military skills for many future leaders. Indeed siege mentality was rampant at the beginning of the Boer War and must have imprinted itself on these men. In one sense the First World War was one long siege but on a vast front hundreds of miles long and in the end there were no real winners. Both Henry Rawlinson and Ian Hamilton, as well as Robert Kekewich, would be present at Rooiwal, the last Boer cavalry charge that effectively ended the Boer War.

During the Siege of Ladysmith the population was about 21,000 of whom 13,800 were troops. There were 7,600 civilians including a scattering of war reporters along with Dr Jameson himself and Cecil Rhodes's brother Frank. The tally of livestock included 4,580 horses, oxen and mules which came in handy when you were a bit hungry.

On the other side there were about 21,000 Boers under Piet Joubert, Louis Botha and Christiaan de Wet. The Commandos besieging Ladysmith were: Pretoria, Irish and German, Lydenburg, Swaziland, Ermelo, Bethel, Carolina, Middleburg, Heildelberg, Wakkerstroom, Krugersdorp, Standerton, Utrecht, Vryheid, Harrismith, Bethlehem, Vrede, Kroonstad and Winburg.

Ladysmith was not a brilliant place to defend as it lay in the bottom of a valley and all the hills which surrounded it were occupied by the Boers, who of course

Siege of Ladysmith – The defence of Caesar's Camp
"Fix bayonets!" R. Caton Woodville

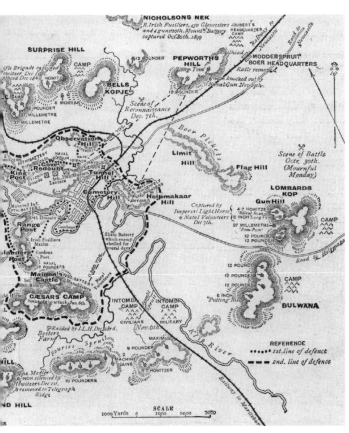

Map of Ladysmith showing perimeter of siege lines and Boer positions etc.

had their artillery including one or two 'Long Toms'. It had a perimeter of fifteen miles. And apart from one or two very sharp raids, it was a relatively gentlemanly siege and the Boers were mostly quite content to just keep lobbing shells into the town whenever they got bored. In the end there were about 850 casualties of whom 227 were killed.

An early agreement between Sir George White and Piet Joubert allowed for one train a day to take wounded and diseased men a few miles down the line to the hospital at Intombi. Of the 583 soldiers who died there, 382 deaths resulted from enteric fever and 109 from dysentery. Disease killed far more than the shelling. Once cured, no soldiers were allowed back into Ladysmith.

Also inside the town there was a small detachment of naval gunners from H.M.S. *Powerful*. They had to haul their guns inland from Durban when their oxen died, and the sailors arrived just before the siege started. A journey of 189 miles. The 4.7 inch guns were called Lady Anne and Princess Victoria. There was another naval brigade with sailors from H.M.S. *Terrible* helping General Redvers Buller with their guns in the Relief of Ladysmith. The sound of various battles of Colenso on the Tugela River could be heard clearly in Ladysmith, so they knew that they had not been totally forgotten.

Early in the siege racing pigeons were used to get important messages out and at one point a photograph of

Boer searchlight used to confuse the enemy signalling

Ladysmith was smuggled out in four sections. Each quarter of the photograph tied to a leg and the four pigeons sent off at 25 minutes intervals. It took them five hours to reach Durban. All four arrived and the photograph was then reconstructed by the intelligence wallahs and sent to Buller's headquarters. There were also telephones, primitive wireless equipment and balloons as well as runners and bicycles.

War correspondents were ten a penny.

Boredom

This small description of how boredom set in is taken from a book called *Kitchener's Sword Arm – The Life and Campaigns of General Sir Archibald Hunter* by Archie Hunter. The General was his great uncle and for many years Kitchener's right hand man. He was bottled up in Ladysmith.

Boredom was a major problem, and when morale sagged, malnutrition and disease took over. Lethargy set in as well as jaundice. The shelling was almost incidental. One or two attacks which Hunter took part in were designed to spike the Boer guns and succeeded in one or two cases. General Hunter later distinguished himself in the Brandwater Basin where over 4,500 Boers were trapped and very wisely surrendered to him.

Alarms

Richard Harding Davis (1864-1916) was an American writer and journalist. He had already covered the Greek-Turkish War of 1897 and Spanish-American War of 1898 which was in effect the tail end of the Cuban War of Independence. Davis became a managing editor of

Robert Harding Davis

Harper's Weekly and as a war correspondent covered the early days of the Boer War and worked for the *New York Herald, The Times* and *Scribner's Magazine*. Davis was a good friend of Theodore Roosevelt. An account of his Boer War experiences then appeared as a book called *With Both Armies*. He later covered the Russo-Japanese War of 1904/05, and the First War with French troops in France and in Salonika.

This account of the shells falling in Ladysmith is taken from his book *Notes from a War Correspondent*. His description of the execution of a Cuban peasant 'Death of Rodriguez' in 1897 is as good as anything that Hemingway produced.

Tied Piper

The piper's son was Major Kenneth Cameron who lived in my own village and he informed me very reliably that his father had played these pipes in the Siege of Ladysmith. He himself had been in the Siege of Malta in 1942 as a searchlight officer. Interestingly searchlights played an important role in the Siege of Ladysmith for relaying messages by morse code from General Buller's headquarters in Frere some thirty miles down the line.

The messages were bounced off the clouds. No doubt the sound of highland pipes kept the Boers amused at breakfast, when taking coffee, dry rusks and chewing on their daily ration of biltong.

Cooking arrangements at General Roberts' HQ Pretoria 1900

Malaria

During the Boer War, disease in the military was a major problem. Out of approximately 55,000 British casualties, only 7,894 were actually killed in action or died of wounds. Around 23,000 wounded and recovered, 13,000 men died of disease, 934 men listed as missing. An additional 10,094 had some form of disease but recovered. Eighty-six soldiers were killed or injured by lightning. One soldier was reportedly eaten by a crocodile at the Usutu River.

Just to put this all into perspective the British casualties during the whole Boer War were almost identical to those on the First Day of the Somme. A very sobering thought. No soldiers as far as we know were killed by crocodiles on the Western Front.

As an example the outbreak of enteric fever (now known as typhoid) was very severe. The Boers had seized the water works supplying Bloemfontein. The troops were supplied from wayside pools or any other source. Some 6,000 soldiers came down with this severe and protracted fever. One hospital with 500 beds had 1,700 sick; death rates soared and as many as fifty men died in one day. The outbreak at Bloemfontein cost the British Army more lives than in the two severest battles of the war.

Of the Boer military casualties in the South African War 9,098 died of whom approximately 4,000 were killed in combat. Approximately 25,000 Boer prisoners were sent overseas.

As far as mosquitos are concerned, the Boer's secret weapon, one is reminded of the line 'For the female of the species is more deadly than the male.' which is taken from Rudyard Kipling. He did in fact write many poems about the Boer War including one on the Mounted Infantry called 'MI'. The line also refers to the female anopholes mosquito which is the one that bites you and thereby transfers the disease. The word anopheles means 'no profit' or 'useless' in Greek. The male mosquito curiously does not like blood and does not bite. They feed on plant nectar...much more civilised.

Scurvy

Having retreated from Dundee, 69th Field Battery was really feeling the pinch at Ladysmith and had to sit the siege out. Their guns were sited at Leicester Post and Rifleman's Post. Rations were clearly running out. Scurvy is of course caused by lack of Vitamin C found in fruit and vegetables. It was a problem in the other two towns that were besieged, Mafeking and Kimberley, as well as

Major Russell and Sister Ross taking wounded on board a hospital train at Orange River Station

in the other camps. Many also must have been suffering from hepatitis, and had that yellowy look. A jaundiced view of the world no doubt. When this was written by Lt Max Chevenix Trench the siege had eight more days to run before Ladysmith was relieved. As in politics a week is a long time.

Cigars

This piece also comes from Richard Harding Davis and is taken from *Notes of a War Correspondent*. A delightful vignette. And as all the other war correspondents who had been bottled up for many months, rode out to file their reports, Davis rode in, and captured the moment exactly. The two officers he describes were escorting Davis to the press censor. They found the censor at his post and a few minutes later 'a signal officer on Convent Hill heliographed my cable to Bulwana, where, six hours after the Boers had abandoned it, Buller's own helios had begun to dance, and they speeded the cable on its long journey to the newspaper office on the Thames Embankment'.

Food Auction Prices

Price of food escalated rapidly towards the end of the siege. Feeding 21,000 people was not easy when you had no idea how long the siege would last. At Christmas 1899 an egg cost a shilling, fresh milk 2 shillings and small potatoes, a shilling each. Whisky was now £5 10s a bottle. Water was rationed to 2 pints a man.
By Tuesday 9 January eggs were 18/- a dozen and potatoes 4/- a pound. Cigarettes – sixpence each.

One of the strange concoctions that was made in Ladysmith was Chevril, like Bovril but made from horses. It was made in the engine shed at the railway workshops. Horse flesh and crushed bones were boiled up in vast cauldrons till they became one large mass of jelly paste. Many liked it and drank it much as one would drink beef tea. It did not catch on after the war.

In November 1899 Queen Victoria was so concerned about her troops that she and the government had commissioned 100,000 tins of chocolate for issue to the soldiers. The chocolate, could be eaten raw or consumed as cocoa, and was sent out in tin boxes each containing half a pound, sufficient to make twelve or sixteen cups. One does not know if the Ladysmith contingent as well as those in Mafeking and Kimberley received their share retrospectively. I hope they did.

Relief at Last

This was no easy matter and Buller's army slogged it out with increasingly high casualties. There had been the Battle of Colenso (15 December 1899), the third and final battle fought during the Black Week. Crossing the Tugela River was no easy matter. Buller's army lost 143 killed, 756 wounded and 220 captured. They also lost ten guns. Boer casualties were only eight killed and thirty wounded. The Boers had once again dug in with well camouflaged lines.

Spion Kop (20-24 January 1900) was another disaster where the British casualties were about 1,500 men. Vaal Krantz (5-7 February 1900) was another small battle where there were another 300 British casualties. A week later they had another go at a different spot and this time it worked. The Battle of Tugela Heights (14-27 February 1900) was still costly with over 2,000 casualties but they made progress by using pontoons and crossing the Tugela River out of sight of the Boers. Something they should have done much earlier. They even used an early form of creeping barrage with the infantry walking behind the moving front. Tactics which were used endlessly in the First War. It was all in the timing. At the end of the battle the Boers retreated and the road to Ladysmith was open.

Around 5 p.m. on 28 February two squadrons of British mounted infantry rode into Ladysmith and ended the siege. Relief all round.

Boers on Spioenkop after the battle, January 1900

The Devons

For the Devon regiment the Relief of Ladysmith was particularly poignant as their 1st Battalion was locked inside Ladysmith and their 2nd Battalion was fighting towards the town with Buller, a Devon general, to meet them. The 1st Battalion had also fought at Elandslaagte. Their description of the sound of Mauser fire is very accurate and the best I could find: 'like the crackle of a piece of gorse in a blazing fire'.

The Devons at Ladysmith facing Pepworth Hill

They played a key part in the Defence of Ladysmith when the Boers tried to take Caesar's Camp. The battle was a Boer night attack and lasted from 3 a.m. till 5 p.m. Losses were heavy on both sides.

One of Richard Harding's well known quotes is: 'The secret of good writing is to say an old thing in a new way or to say a new thing in an old way'.

Part 4

Guerrilla War

Bed and No Breakfast

They had been out somewhere else
He and another chap

And it was night time and they came
To this deserted farmhouse

And they decided they would go to bed
Didn't see a soul.

Well during the night
The other fellow got up and went downstairs

Came back got into bed again.
But when daylight came he found

He had gone into the wrong room
And he had got into bed with a dead Dutchman.

Par for the course. Sweet dreams.
No doubt the Dutchman owned the place.

**Kathleen Bennett talking about her by her father
Harry Howlett 18th Hussars**

Hunting

My Dear Jack,

You would love to be out here now.
We are about 16 miles from Vryheid
In the best game country I have ever seen.

There are quantities of buck, duck
and two kinds of bustard
Besides a few hares and quantities of pigeon.

Game laws are non-existent
But game is wild and if one goes far out
Boers spring upon you unawares to your detriment.

Boers out shooting squirrels

That fellow Newland whom they caught
A fortnight ago had to pay £30 for his horse,
Carbine and saddle which they took from him.

Otherwise they treated him like a brother.
About that *sjambok*, I sent it home to Mother
With a letter to forward it to Olive Walker.

It seems that the letter was caught in a mail convoy
By the Boers and the family have retained the *sjambok*.
Can you send it on with profuse apologies.

I will send you another as soon as possible...
I will also send you some Boer tobacco as soon as I can.
Everyone smokes it out here. It is very cool...

Love to all
Your affectionate brother
Max

28 October 1900
Lt Max Chevenix Trench R.A.

Night Visitors

The Boers attacked at 2.15 a.m.
Rushed the Mounted Infantry camp
And were among the tents
While the men were still looking

For their guns in the dark.
Their horses had been stampeded
And been either shot or captured.
They had a few men killed

And thirty taken prisoner.
The Boers had also captured
The reserve ammunition
Of twenty thousand rounds.

Vryheid April 1901
Lt Max Chevenix Trench R.A.

Jones's Hotel – The Customers

Ventersburg was not destroying incriminating documents
nor driving weary burghers from its solitary street.
It was making them welcome at Jones's Hotel.

The sun had sunk an angry crimson,
the sure sign of a bloody battle on the morrow,
and a full moon had turned the dusty street, and the veldt
into which it disappeared, into 'a field of snow'.

The American scouts had halted at Jones's Hotel,
and the American proprietor was giving them drinks free.
Their cowboy spurs jingled on the floor of the bar-room,
on the boards of the verandas, on the stone floor of the kitchen,
and in the billiard-room, where they were playing pool
as joyously as though the English were not ten miles away.

Grave, awkward burghers rode up, each in a cloud of dust,
and leaving his pony to wander in the street
and his rifle in a corner, shook hands
with every one solemnly, and asked for coffee.
Italians of Garibaldi's red-shirted army,
Swedes and Danes in semi-uniform,
Frenchman in high boots and great sombreros,
Germans with the sabre cuts on their cheeks
that had been given them at the university,
and Russian officers smoking tiny cigarettes
crowded the little dining room,

Anyone for a shot of whisky?

and by the light of a smoky lamp
talked in many tongues of Spion Kop, Sannah's Post,
Fourteen Streams, and the battle on the morrow.

They were sun-tanned, dusty, stained,
and many of them with wounds in bandages.
They came from every capital of Europe,
and as each took his turn around the crowded table,
they drank to the health of every nation, save one.
When they had eaten they picked up the pony's bridle
from the dust and melted into the moonlight
with a wave of the hand and a "Good luck to you".
There were no bugles to sound 'Boots and Saddles' for them,
no sergeants to keep them in hand,
no officers to pay for their rations and issue orders.

Each was his own officer, his conscience was his bugle-call,
he gave himself orders. They were all equal, all friends:
the cowboy and the Russian Prince,
the French socialist from La Villette or Montmartre,
with a red sash around his velveteen breeches,
and the little French nobleman from the Cercle Royal
who had never before felt the sun,
except when he had played lawn tennis on the Isle de Puteaux.
Each had his bandolier and rifle;
each was minding his own business,
which was the business of all –
to try and save the independence of a free people.

These foreigners were not soldiers of fortune,
for the soldier of fortune fights for gain.
These men receive no pay, no emolument, no reward.
They were the few who dared do
what the majority of their countrymen
in Europe thought.

At Jones's Hotel that night, at Ventersburg,
it was as though a jury composed of men
from all of Europe and the United States
had gathered in judgment on the British nation.

Richard Harding Davis Ventersburg May 1900

The Proprietress

The original Jones, the proprietor of Jones's Hotel, had fled.
The man who succeeded him was also a refugee,
and the present manager was an American from Cincinnati.

He had never before kept a hotel,
but he confided to me that it was not a bad business,
as he found that on each drink sold
he made a profit of a hundred per cent.

The proprietress was a lady from Brooklyn,
her husband, another American,
was a prisoner with Cronjé at St Helena.

She was in considerable doubt
as to whether she ought to run before the British arrived,
or wait and chance being made a prisoner.

She said she would prefer to escape,
but what with standing on her feet all day
in the kitchen preparing meals for hungry burghers
and foreign volunteers, she was too tired to get away.

Richard Harding Davis Ventersburg May 1900

Tulip Grass

Lieutenants Lichtenberg and Purdey
Rejoined at Wonderfontein,
the former officer now practically cured
of his dangerous wound,
having made a very rapid recovery.

An accumulation of many mails
and our refitting arrangements
gave us plenty to do
for the next few days we were halted.
We received eighty remounts,
but had to send sixty horses into Middleburg,
as they were useless
for further work for some time to come.

Besides these some eighty horses of
'B' Squadron picked up some tulip grass
whilst they were out grazing
and out of this number seven died,
and twenty-three were so ill
that they had to be left behind,
while the remainder were useless
for work for some time to come.

Tulip grass at that time of the year
Was a most dangerous herb,
hard to distinguish,
without a careful examination

from the early shoots of the young grass
which began to come up
from the centre of the valleys in the spring.

All animals would greedily devour it
as a change from the dry burnt up stuff
they had been subsisting on for so long,
and in a few hours its poisonous effect,
soon told fatally alike, on horse, cattle and mules.

4-8 September 1901 Major Charles Burnett 18th Hussar

Cow gun and oxen crossing the Zand River 1900

Dear Diary

July 2nd 1901

Wind. Dust. Vile. Checked stores.
Dust. More Dust. After Lunch
Walked up to see progress
On Naval Hill Road. Imperceptible.

It is a slow job getting out big iron-stone rocks
First splitting them with dynamite.
Wind gone down
Tea. Read. Dinner. Bed.

Washing

July 3rd 1901

Hard Frost. Sponge very little used.
But first rate missile.

Warm hands on porridge bowl.
Then warm tummy with porridge.

What should we do
Without Quaker Oats?

Lt Christopher Chevenix Trench
No 7 Field Company Royal Engineers
Bloemfontein

More oats

Ambush

It was the wire tap that did for them
A Boer telephone engineer –
Ridden 40 miles or more then shinned up a pole
Listened in with his stethoscope,

To H.Q. the message loud and clear
A picking too good to miss. Orders for
No. 3 Flying Column on escort duty
Convoy of heavily laden carts back to base.

No. 3 Flying Column specialised in night raids
No. 3 Flying Column was Colonel Benson,
Kitchener's very best man for the job.
Handpicked, he terrorised the Boers

Just as they had terrorised
The British troops.
Played them at their own game
Outwitted them many times over.

Often caught them at dawn
Meticulous planning, eagle eyed scouts
Intelligence was always excellent.
A real thorn in the side of the Boers

Was Colonel Benson. Had Louis Botha
Really rattled, his men were getting edgy
And on the run. So when he got wind
Of their route, he went in for the kill.

Summoned 800 of his best troops
By heliograph, a flash in the pan.
They rode like hell, the weather was bad
The wagons were stuck in the drift

Like wolves they went for the rearguard
Cut them off and then cut them up again.
Charged from both sides, shooting from the saddle
Bitter fighting. No quarter given or taken.

In twenty minutes the rear guard
Outnumbered four to one, annihilated.
Shot in the arm and then the stomach,
Colonel Benson himself went down.

Died of wounds the very next day.
But the convoy and most of the troops
Were saved. It worried Kitchener no end.
That Benson's column was 'smashed up'.

Bodies were stripped of their clothing
The Boers took what they could
Men were buried where they lay.
Botha licked his lips, went back to his lair.

Bakenlaagte 30 October 1901

Blowing up Railway Bridges

The crossing of the drifts
at the two rivers was almost
as difficult a task as
the overtaking of our ever retreating foes.

The railway bridges over both these streams
had been blown up by dynamite:
some of the stone piers were shattered,
and some of the iron girders hurled
all atwist into the watery depths beneath;

here and there culverts had similarly been destroyed,
and at many a point the very rails
had been torn by explosives
till they looked like a pair of upturned arms
imploring help from heaven.

We noticed, however, when we got
into the Transvaal that the Transvaalers
took pity on their own portion of the line,
and studiously refrained from shattering it.

Some of them were probably shareholders.

Edward Lowry Chaplain to the Guards' Brigade

1st Coldstreams washing in the Vaal River.
In the distance the blown railway bridge

Travelling 3rd Class

Duel purpose

Last Gentleman's War

My father always said the Boer War
Was the last gentleman's war
That was ever fought
Because they didn't fight on a Sunday

And they'd call a truce
To collect their wounded
Exchange medical supplies
And bury their dead.

On Patrol – Looking for more oats

Now on one occasion he was on a patrol
And this very young lad rode up,
He said he had got long fair curls,
I always remember him with his white flag.

He wanted medical supplies,
So he was blindfolded
Taken behind the lines
Given what supplies he needed

And what they could spare
Taken back and sent on his way.
So we go onto the First World War
And the South Africans had come into the war

And my father had gone into the mess for a drink
Whether it was a dugout mess I don't know
But there were some of these
South Africans leaning against the bar.

One of them looked round
And said to my father "I know you!"
And it was this young lad grown up
Almost unbelievable isn't it?

**Kathleen Bennett talking about her father,
Harry Howlett, 18th Hussars**

Officers – East Yorkshire Regiment – First beer in four months

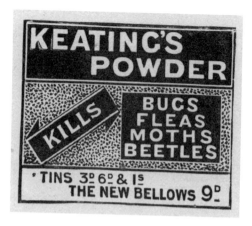

Dog's Life

I am very sorry for Loyal Boer Farmers
Theirs must be a dog's life.
Quite apart from the chance they stand

Of losing all their stock in a lump to the Boers
Or little by little to the T.A. (Mounted Variety)
They have the following pleasures always with them:

Their horses are always taken by the Remounts
They can only keep two or three
by special sanction of the P.M.

They must have a permit to buy
or sell cattle of any kind
Another permit to buy provisions,

The amount being strictly limited.
They must get a pass to be off their farms
Another to be on their farms.

A pass to travel by rail
Another to travel by road
A different pass for each journey

Altogether it is a wonder
One hears
So very little complaining.

19 September 1901
Lt Christopher Chevenix Trench R.E.   Bloemfontein

Boer farmer's wife

Brandwater Basin – Surrender

We were not allowed to talk with the prisoners.
They appeared eager to do so. They seemed
Most anxious to glean some information
As to their ultimate destination.

The prisoners, one and all, looked neat
And, for the most part, fairly clean.
They did not appear as if they suffered hardships
Beyond the ordinary ones attendant upon long treks.

Of saddles and horses
They had a good supply,
And were better mounted –
If on smaller horses – than we were.

They were in civilian clothes,
Without uniform or uniformity,
But coloured blankets and shawls
Lent an occasional bright touch to their assemblage.

Some few were belted,
But, apart from these particulars,
There was little to mark
That they had been a military body.

They held about them more of the appearance
Of the hunter than of the soldier, and many
Of the older, big-bearded men reminded me of
Venerable pioneers of the western prairies of America.

As they halted in the road, holding in check
Their restless little ponies, a tall, grave-looking man
With a narrow, long, sandy beard, rode down their line,
Shaking hands here and there in the ranks.

As he turned at the head of the little column
Nearly every man lifted –
For a moment – his right hand
And ejaculated a single word.

I asked what it was,
And I was told that Prinsloo
Was saying goodbye,
And that the word was "General".

30 July 1900
Trooper William Corner, Middlesex Imperial Yeomanry

*A British Field gun captured at Colenso being used by the Boers
at the Siege of Ladysmith Feb 1900*

Prisoners of War

Met a Boer general yesterday
Aged only 24 or 25
Surrendered with his men.
Lean, wiry, tanned to a whisker
Never forget the look in their eyes.

Very odd that feeling of being in the saddle
With a carbine over your knee
Escorting a whole commando
Two hundred men, or what is left of them
Knowing that every one of them

Boer prisoners after Paardeberg 28 Feb 1900

Is a far better shot than you will ever be.
They could slip through your fingers
In a single night
Ran rings round the staff officers.
The foresight saga.

Their clothes were ragged,
Their hair was long
Their silence was deafening.
Only the sound of the horses's hooves
And the dust pittering on behind.

Trooper Theodore Fleming
Bethune's Mounted Infantry

Shell shocked

Cornelis Van Gogh

It must have been difficult for him
with an elder brother like Vincent,
all wrapped up in paint and canvas
absinthe and the floozies
of Sam Remy and Auvers-sur-Oise
and Theodore wrapped up
in his world of art dealing,
and syphilis. Framed again
the collectors not quite sure
what it was they had just bought.

Not a world for Cornelis, the odd one out
he did not choose to go off the rails
but stayed on track
became a railway engineer.
Mines needed such men
engineers were king
gold had to have its apprentices.
Fom far and wide the tracks ran wild
from Pretoria to Lourenço Marques
Mozambique was on his map
Gold one way, arms, people, explosives the other.

True he had seen the insides of Lincoln
railway sheds, but here Cornucopia
had got him in their grasp,
making engines, what he knew best.

He even joined the Zarps
when Dr Jameson was caught
with his trousers down.

There was no doubting his loyalties –
he became an ambulance driver
in the Hollander Korps
the Dutch Commando
a risky enough business
as weapons and ammunition
were sometimes smuggled onto the front line
during a truce, in ambulances.

Cornelis Van Gogh

He himself was caught near Kroonstad
March 1900, captured,
then moved to a military hospital
fever set in and by mid April
he had departed this world.

A single gun shot wound
might just have been self inflicted,
might not. They said it was accidental,
may just have happened when he was captured.
These things do occur, you know,
and the wound may have gone bad.

The fever must have taken its toll.
Maybe it was just malaria picked up
from working on the railway
as deadly as syphilis they say.
The picture darkens
as the shovel sends the earth
back down onto his dark
wrapped up engineered body.

I wonder what Vincent
would have thought of it all,
and what sort of fiery paintings
he would have made
had he been there with his easel.

Nurses – Between the Lines

Troop train outside Pietermaritzburg
No doubt fresh from Durban
A whole carriage load of nurses,
Keen to do their bit for King and Country,

All night parked up in a siding
And us kipped out
On the embankment opposite
With only a blanket under the stars.

And our imagination, which to be honest
Ran wild that night, for it was many months
Since we had seen a pretty face
And heard a pretty voice

We had lived pretty rough
And survived by the skin of our teeth
Hardened by sun and dust
We had in most matters gone native.

But as the train pulled out next morning
Those rosy cheeked nurses leaned out
And waved to us and smiled
Their starched linen and long blue-grey dresses

A sight for sore eyes, young and shapely.
But we killed ourselves laughing,
For some bright wag had scrawled
Below the carriage windows

Where, alas, they could not see
In chalk letters three feet high
'OFFICER'S REMOUNTS'
Curves to die for if matron had her way.

We had lived pretty rough…

Trooper Theodore Fleming Bethune's Mounted Infantry

Hospital train No 4 – Matron on the lookout

Enteric Fever

Nothing much we could do for them,
Fever and rose spots on the chest
Rather like typhus
Nothing much we could do.

By the second week
Emaciated and semi-delirious
The fever used to rise
In the afternoon.

Feeding was a problem
Used to give them milk,
Diarrhoea like pea soup
The smell was not so good.

Usually they just faded away,
A swig of brandy or what ever else
You had to hand. About half died.
Nothing much we could do.

I did like the thunder storms
And even took a camera.
You get used to being under canvas
By the end I ran my own ward.

Edith Monck-Mason

Below the Belt

I heard the story from my maternal grandmother,
Maria Elizabeth Van Rensburg Lourens.
She and my paternal grandmother,
Susara Magdalena Wilhelmina Grobler
lived on adjacent farms near Villiers
in the Orange Free State, and both their husbands
were away and fighting somewhere...
unfortunately, I have no details of that.

The English commander or whatever he was,
came with ox wagons to take them
to a concentration camp near Bethlehem
(I am not sure of this... maybe another one)
and Maria Elizabeth with three children were loaded first.

Susara was an attractive woman
according to Maria Elizabeth
and the commander tried to seduce her
and she roughly kicked him
where she maybe thought the origin
of the problem came from.

In his agony, he took his revenge
by giving her five minutes to load
whatever she needed for the camp –
which was like a death sentence.

I do not know how many children
she had with her and how many died
but Maria had three children
of whom the two youngest died.

Every year, on commemoration day,
she would dress in total black Voortrekker dress
to remember the pain and loss
she endured and they remained loyal
to resistance against the English
whilst the Groblers joined Jan Smuts
and his philosophy of holism.

Saar Steenkamp

Boer family on the move
having been evicted from their farm

Emily Hobhouse – Bloemfontein
Excerpts from her letters and reports

January 1901

Imagine the heat outside the tents
And the suffocation inside!

We sat on khaki blankets, rolled up on Mrs B's tent;
And the suns blazed through the single canvas,
and the flies lay thick and black on everything;
no chair, no table, nor any room for such;
Only a deal box, standing on its end served as a wee pantry.

In this tiny tent lived Mrs B's five children
(three quite grown up) and a little servant girl.
Many tents have more occupants.

Boer families at a concentration camp in Eshowe in Zululand

On wet nights the water streams down
through the canvas and comes flooding in,
as it knows how to do in this country,
under the flap of the tent,
and wets their blankets as they lie on the ground.

While we sat there a snake came in.
They said it was a puff adder, very poisonous,
so they all ran out
And I attacked the creature with my parasol.

I could not bear to think the thing should be at large
in a community mostly sleeping on the ground.

After a struggle I wounded it, and then a man
Came with a mallet and finished it off.

March 1901

There was a scarcity of essential provisions.
The accommodation was wholly inadequate.
When the eight, ten or twelve people
who lived in the bell tent were squeezed into it
to find shelter against the heat of the sun, the dust or the rain,
there was no room to stir and the air in the tent
was beyond description, even though
the flaps were rolled up properly and fastened.
Soap was an article that was not dispensed.
The water supply was inadequate.
No bedstead or mattress was procurable.

Emily Hobhouse

Fuel was scarce and had to be collected
from the green bushes on the slopes of the kopjes
by the people themselves.

The rations were extremely meagre and when,
as I frequently experienced, the actual quantity dispensed
fell short of the amount prescribed, it simply meant famine.

April 1901

In many instances I was an eyewitness
of what took place. I saw families huddled up
close to the railway line near Warrenton and Fourteen Streams.

I saw an overcrowded train crawling along to Kimberley
throughout a whole long night.

I saw people, old and young, bundled in open trucks
under a scorching sun near a station building
without anything to eat.

At midnight they were transported
to empty tents where they groped about in the dark,
looking for their little bundles.

They went to sleep without any provision
having been made for them
and without anything to eat or to drink.
I saw crowds of them along railway lines
in bitterly cold weather, in pouring rain –
hungry, sick, dying and dead.

My first visit to the Bloemfontein camp
after the lapse of some weeks, was a great shock to me.
The population had redoubled
and had swallowed up the results of improvements
that had been effected.

Disease was on the increase
and the sight of the people made the impression of utter misery.
Illness and death had left their marks
on the faces of the inhabitants.

Many that I had left hale and hearty, of good appearance
and physically fit, had undergone
such a change that I could hardly recognize them.

Emily Hobhouse

Notes: Part 4
Guerrilla War

Bed and No Breakfast

From 1900 onwards after the set piece battles and the capture of Bloemfontein and Pretoria, the war gradually became one of guerrilla tactics and attrition. The Boer commandos often ran rings round the British troops and patrols were long and often the only place of rest would be an isolated or abandoned farmhouse. Both sides played a game of hide and seek, and the role of the cavalry as mounted infantry and scouts became more and more important. There were a vast number of irregular units many of them recruited from other parts of

Capture of a Boer farm at Dewetsdorp by Bethune's M.I.

Africa, Australia, New Zealand and Canada.

Farms were often used not just for rest but as ambush sites by one side or the other. There were even cases of soldiers dressed as women to lure the enemy in, thinking it was safe. Sometimes the Boers wore British uniform either to fool the British to get close and shoot them or simply because they had no other clothes to wear. This was a bitter war where many farm houses were burnt, crops destroyed and cattle raided.

Hunting

Once the Siege of Ladysmith had been lifted, the battery slowly recovered then headed off to Laing's Nek and Amersfoort. A little bit of light shooting for the pot never went amiss. One has to keep one's eye in.

Sjambok is a leather whip traditionally made from the hide of an adult hippopotamus or rhinoceros. They were

Keeping his eye in

useful for moving cattle and for warding off snakes and dogs. Boer generals carried them as a symbol of rank, rather than a firearm. Not doubt they had 'street cred' back home in England with the riding fraternity.

Night Visitors

Just another little skirmish by Louis Botha. Tit for tat. Food, ammunition and clothing and horses were the usual prey. For the Boers, taking prisoners was a bit of a liability because they would have to feed them and they would slow them down on campaign. They often just de-bagged them.

Jones's Hotel

Ventersburg was occupied by British Forces on 10 May 1900 so this description of the Jones's Hotel drinking den may well have occurred on the evening of 9 May 1900. The Boers fought a good rearguard action along the Zand River but were eventually outflanked. Kroonstad was taken four days later on 14 May and Mafeking relieved on 17 May 1900.

There were by all accounts several cases of white flag shootings around Kroonstad and Ventersburg and this is exactly the time and place that Cornelis Van Gogh was shot and wounded when he surrendered. The town of Ventersburg was later burnt, but how badly and by whom and for what reason is not exactly clear. Certainly the Boers threatened to do it but may have had other things on their mind when retreating. One hopes the Jones's Hotel remained intact with its liquor supplies, and one wonders whether the hard working and brave proprietress stayed on to welcome the British troops.

Black scouts – a listening post with blockhouses behind

Tulip Grass

Horses were sometimes ridden to death in the heat. It was a cruel war for animals and remounts had to be brought in from all over the world.

Tulip grass is very poisonous to grazing animals and goes under a variety of names. *Moraea miniata Andrew* or *Homeria miniata* (Andrews) Sweet otherwise known as 'Two-Leaved Cape Tulip' or *Rooitulp* in South Africa. It has a green bulb which looks very attractive in the winter when the old grasses have dried up. Animals that are not used to it such as horses brought in from abroad tend to guzzle the leaves. A kilo can kill a cow. It effects the nervous system and heart a bit like *digitalis*, which gives symptoms such as bloat, nervousness and immobility, even paralysis. Death occurs from heart failure. Local animals learn to avoid it early on in their lives.

Lieutenant Lichtenberg was a very brave man and had acquitted himself well at Massif's Drift on 30 June 1901 where he was dangerously wounded. He was awarded a DSO. Although not a poem in any sense it still gives a very real feel of what it was like in a lull between fighting. This extract is taken from *The 18th Hussars in South Africa* by Major Charles Burnett.

Dear Diary

These are the entries for Lt Christopher Chevenix Trench who was an officer in No. 7 Field Company Royal Engineers based at Bloemfontein. They helped to make the pontoon bridge across the Tugela River, out of sight of the Boers and this made a flanking attack possible. One section of their company was bottled up in Kimberley during the siege. Their normal duties were road building, bridge building, fortifications, water supply and of course blowing things up. Without porridge oats life would have been even more unbearable.

Ambush

Ambush was the normal Boer tactic. Ever since the Battle of Kraaipan, it had worked many times, even on a large scale against a full blown brigade or two. But you had to know the lie of the land and you had to be very flexible and know when to break off an action. Here the Boers had exceptionally good intelligence simply by listening into the telephone line. Coded messages were used but the codes were often very simple. False messages were sent and false trails laid. There were many spies on either side and women played a large part in the early stages of the war passing on information about troop movements. But once the farms were cleared they could do little to help their men.

The Boer who tapped the line was a field telephone

Ambush at Bakenlaagte 30 October 1901

engineer called Piet Jooste whose day job had been Chairman of the Diamond Control Board. He simply tapped the wire with his vibrator and listened in. Remarkably, the message intercepted was from Colonel Benson, informing Lord Kitchener at Standerton that he was 'Leaving Middelburg for the High Veld on 20 October with a large convoy and 2,200 men.' Heliographs did the rest as Louis Botha gathered the pack together.

For the Boers this action was very risky, committing so many commandos in single raid, but it paid off. British losses in the action were 238 killed and wounded, and 120 taken prisoner. About a quarter of the column's original strength. Boer casualties were reportedly about 190, including sixty killed.

British losses were worst on Gun Hill, where the defence was practically annihilated; only seventeen of the 190 troops there got away unwounded. Of the Scottish Horse, thirty-three were killed and another fifty-seven were wounded. The secret as always was surprise and in this case bad weather helped the Boers. There was a thunderstorm. The convoy became spread out so the covering troops were also spread out.

Even though he was their enemy, Colonel George Elliott Benson was admired and respected by the Boers for his skills as a soldier. Originally from Northumberland, he had served in the Sudan and in Egypt and was at Modder River and Magersfontein. After his death they erected a handsome statue to him in Hexham which is still there today. His usually excellent intelligence came from a man called Colonel Aubrey Wools-Sampson who had been a gold miner and a prominent Uitlander and set up the Imperial Light Horse. He also had some excellent native scouts, without whom the British would often have been blind. If the scouts were caught by the Boers they were often shot on the spot.

One other man who died in this action was L/Cpl G. Herbert Housman, of 'E' Company, 4th Battalion, King's Royal Rifles. He was the youngest brother of the poet, A.E. Housman who wrote *A Shropshire Lad*. This was published in 1896 and is concerned with young men's death. A case of real life imitating art. Like Kipling, his words came back to haunt him.

Colonel George Elliott Benson

One reason why this action is included is that another great uncle of mine called James Scott Crowden was a trooper in the 2nd Scottish Horse and would have been there, though he never spoke about it. He was a marine engineer who left his ship in Cape Town and went soldiering. In the First War whilst serving as Chief Engineer on the *SS Kabinga* with a cargo of jute, he was captured by the cruiser *Emden* in the Bay of Bengal but later released.

Much has been written on this action at Bakenlaagte and it is very well documented.

Last Gentleman's War

Another anecdote told to me by Kathleen Bennett whose father Private Harry Howlett was in the 18th Hussars. On one level as this story shows the Boer War was very gentlemanly. The Boers did not fight on Sundays and there were often many truces to allow ambulances onto the battle field to tend to the wounded or, as in this case, to give the enemy bandages and wound dressings etc. Occasionally there were prisoner exchanges, though towards the end of the war there were cases of prisoners being shot. Often the Boers were very loathe to take prisoners and would simply strip them of all clothing, weapons, horses, ammunition and food and then send the men ignominiously back to their lines. Walking for several days under the scorching sun was no joke even in your long-johns.

What this story shows is that many Boers after a few years were prepared to fight alongside Britain in the First War. What is less well known is that something in the region of about 6,000 Boers were, towards the end of the Boer War fighting on the British side. They were often disillusioned with the hell-raising antics of some of their commando leaders.

Dog's Life

This small extract shows how difficult things must have been for the loyal Boers in the Cape. Some of them then fought with the Boers and were then labelled Cape Rebels. If they were caught as some were, they were executed. Lt Christopher Chevenix Trench obviously sympathised with them and their plight. Six months later he lay dying of enteric fever. He died on 13 April 1902.

His brother Lt Max Chevenix Trench survived the Boer War and was mentioned in dispatches. In 1908 he was on the Blue Nile Patrol. When the First World War broke out he went to France with the British Expeditionary Force and served on the Divisional staff as a major. But his luck ran out when he, and six other senior staff officers, were killed by a single German shell on 31 October 1914. Location: the grounds of a French country house called Chateau de la Hooge near Ypres. Hooge is a small village on the Menin Road, two miles east of Ypres. This was during the First Battle of Ypres when the British line was nearly broken.

Brandwater Basin – Surrender

The Brandwater Basin was a horseshoe valley system sandwiched between the Roodebergen and Wittebergen. There were at least five passes leading into it or for that matter out of it: Retief's Nek, Slabbert's Nek, Generaal's Nek, Kommando Nek, Naauwpoort Nek and at the far end Golden Gate. It was also on the border of Basutoland. About 8,000 Boers, what was left of the Orange Free State army and the De Wet's commandos were sheltering in there because of the green pasture. They wanted a rest and time to recuperate their horses. But Archie Hunter had other ideas. He was based at Bethlehem. The star on his horizon was a curious one. De Wet outwitted him and managed to escape, by the skin of his teeth over Slabbert's Nek, with about 3,000 men and President Steyn of the Bloemfontein conference, in tow. But that still left a sizeable bag. The passes were all sealed off and they slowly entered, meeting opposition at Retief's Nek. Much of the grass on the tops had been burnt. It made it easier to pick out men crossing it. Slowly the noose tightened and the Boers were squeezed into a trap. Most of the British troops were Scottish and included the Highland Brigade and the Lovat's Scouts. They relished being in the mountains. It was a remarkable piece of coordination as they were reliant on messages by courier, which meant riding hell for leather on horseback. Even heliographs were not always secure as the Boers, if they were in the right position, could read the signals. And you needed good weather. Radio was in its infancy.

The remaining Boers eventually realised that they had been trapped and offered to surrender without a real fight. General Prinsloo saw no point in wasting life unnecessarily. In the circumstances a very wise decision. They had after all been abandoned by Christaan de Wet and President Steyn. It was an honourable surrender and General Archibald Hunter allowed the Boers to keep their covered wagons and oxen.

Surrender at Brandwater Basin

In all 4,314 men surrendered. Three guns were re-captured which had originally been captured at Saana's post, as well as 2,800 head of cattle, 4,000 sheep, and between 5,000 and 6,000 good horses. Two million rounds of ammunition were also destroyed. Not a bad haul. On par with Paarderberg, when Cronjé threw in the towel. The surrender took many days and the prisoners were eventually shipped off to prison camps in Ceylon. The cost to life on both sides had been minimal. A real blessing.

The moving description comes from Trooper William Corner, and his book *The Story of the 34th Company (Middlesex) Imperial Yeomanry* (London, 1902).

Prisoners of War

This anecdote was told to me by Trooper Theodore Fleming of Bethune's Mounted Infantry. This must have been right at the end of the war. The Boers who stuck it out were called 'bitter enders'. Indeed the Boer camp was very divided between those that knew they could not win the war and those that struggled on against the odds. It must have been incredibly difficult for the commandos who knew that their families were in camps and that they were getting less rations because they were out on patrol.

Boers that surrendered were called *hensoppers*, i.e. those who had put their hands up. In some cases the Boers who realised the war was hopeless, actually joined the British irregular units and these were called 'joiners'.

Peace was always round the corner but the timing of it was crucial for both sides. There was even a Burghers Peace Committee made up of men of influence who had surrendered and had come to realise that the war was unwinnable. In December 1900, members of this committee had a meeting with Kitchener who gave them temporary freedom to go back to their own commandos to talk about peace terms. The chairman of the committee Meyer de Kock and at least two others were court-martialled and shot as collaborators and traitors by Boer firing squads. Rough justice, shooting the messenger. Others were lucky to get back to British lines alive.

In September 1901 the British raised two units from Boer Commandos, they were called 'Joiners'. So there were *hensoppers*, 'joiners' and 'bitter enders'.

The 'bitter enders' could not handle prisoners because they had nowhere to send them and could not feed them or afford men to guard them, or look after the wounded, because they had so little of their own, so they simply stripped the British soldiers and then set them free, to walk back to the nearest barracks or outpost.

In the end about 25,000 Boer prisoners were sent abroad. It was too risky to keep them in South Africa. At first they were kept on ships and then they were sent overseas. First they were sent to prison camps in St Helena which took about five thousand prisoners. A similar number were sent to Ceylon. Other camps were set up in Bermuda and India. Some Boers who had escaped to Mozambique ended up being interned in Portugal. In Ceylon five prisoners escaped by swimming to a Russian ship in Colombo harbour and went back home via the Crimea and Holland where they saw Kruger.

One high profile prisoner was Piet Cronjé who had surrendered with his commando at Paardeberg with 4,150 men on 27 February 1900. He was sent to St Helena and his wife who had fought alongside him was allowed to accompany him.

More of Cronjé's men as prisoners

One the other side, one high profile British prisoner captured by the Boers was Lord Methuen himself who was wounded and captured, by General de la Rey's commando, at Tweebosch on 7 March 1902. After the war they became good friends and Lord Methuen helped mend the fences with the new South Africa. Or more realistically take them down.

Cornelis Van Gogh

Cor or Cornelis or Cornelius Van Gogh was born in Holland in 1867 fourteen years after his brother Vincent and ten years after his brother Theo, so there was quite a large gap between them. Most people these days do not even know of his existence or that he had such an interesting life. He decided to have a career as a railway engineer. After training in Helmond and Lincoln he went out to South Africa, the same year Vincent died. It may well be that Vincent's death 'released' him to go there. Cor worked for the Netherlands South African Railway Company and for the Cornucopia Gold Company near

Johannesburg. One of his friends who went out to South Africa in the same year was an artist called Frans Oerder who was the same age as him and came from Rotterdam. When on hard times Frans even had a job as a house decorator and painted telegraph poles on the same railway line that Cor was working on to Delagoa Bay.

When war broke out in 1899 Cor Van Gogh joined the Hollanderkorps, a Dutch commando unit under Cmdt Blignaut. He was an ambulance driver and was captured near Kroonstad in March 1900, and may well have been wounded. The official report stated it was an accidental shooting. Others believe he died of malaria or tuberculosis.

Certainly he fell ill and was put in a military hospital in Brandfort where he died on 14 April 1900. He was buried in an unmarked grave. Some people say that he committed suicide. Not so easy in a hospital. What is more likely is that he was wounded accidentally when surrendering which often happened if there was a misunderstanding. White flags were not always trusted. If he then developed a fever like enteric fever he did not stand much of a chance. In all probability it was malaria which he could easily have picked up when working on the railways.

His friend Frans Oerder was commissioned by Paul Kruger to be the official war artist for the Boers and survived the war. Sadly very few of his sketches survive. Apparently he was working in a school in the Transvaal and had his pictures on the walls when the school burnt down and his unique record was destroyed. A few of his Magersfontein pictures have survived; some are housed in the War Museum, Bloemfontein, and nine sketches were put up for sale at Sotheby's, Johannesburg in 1975.

Nurses - Between the Lines

At the outbreak of the war, the Army Nursing Service consisted of a Lady Superintendent, eighteen Superintendent Sisters and fifty-six Sisters to serve the principal military hospitals in Britain and abroad. By the time the Boer War ended in South Africa there were 200 hospitals, seven hospital trains and eight hospital ships. Four of the trains worked from Cape Town, two in Natal and one from East London. One of them, was donated by Princess Christian, the third daughter of Queen Victoria and named after her. It was the first train to enter Ladysmith after the Relief. It was lavishly equipped and

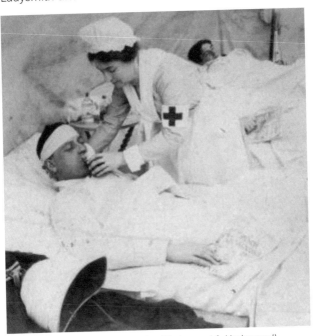

Rather smart Field hospital Tugela. (Underwood & Underwood)

highly spoken of by everyone who worked in it. The hospital train was specifically constructed for the British Central Red Cross Committee. It cost £14,000 and consisted of seven carriages. The Red Cross Society financed another ambulance train which was built and equipped in the East London railway yards.

The demand for nurses was so great that by 1902 a permanent military nursing service was founded – Queen Alexandra's Imperial Military Nursing Service (Q.A.I.M.N.S.). A great many of the original nurses had gone out there under their own steam. There was even a private hospital train. In the end about 1,400 trained nurses went to the Boer War from the UK and about another six hundred went from Australia, New Zealand and Canada.

Nursing sisters had been sent to the First Boer War and later to the Egyptian Campaign in 1882. During the Sudan War they served as nurses in hospital ships on the Nile as well as the Citadel in Cairo. Florence Nightingale would have approved.

Tending the wounded under fire was also a hazardous operation. At least six officers in the R.A.M.C. won the Victoria Cross during the Boer War including Captain Martin Leake, who was one of the very few people to ever win the Victoria Cross twice. Once at Vlakfontein in 1902 and again in Belgium in 1914.

This raucous account of the nurses on a troop train comes once more from Trooper Theodore Fleming of Bethune's Mounted Infantry.

Enteric Fever

Enteric fever or typhoid was a real killer both in the British hospitals and in the concentration camps. Patients usually died within two or three weeks, sometimes a lot less. Of the 13,139 soldiers who died of disease in the Boer War at least half would have been from enteric fever. Enteric is often waterborne. About twenty nurses also died of enteric fever. Sadly the poet Gerard Manley Hopkins and the novelist Arnold Bennett both died of this disease, though not in the Boer War. Bennett had rather foolishly deliberately drunk a glass of water in a Paris hotel to prove it was safe.

Edith Monck-Mason was one of those stalwart nurses for whom the Empire and the Boer War meant work. Her father had died when she was very young. He had been in the Bombay Civil Service. She trained as a nurse at St Bartholomew's Hospital, and served and throughout the Boer War. She also took a camera with her and produced a book of photographs called *The South African Album*. Her younger brother Captain Roger Monck-Mason also served in the Boer War and was an officer in the Royal Munster Fusiliers.

In 1903, after war had ended, Edith joined the Queen Alexandra's Imperial Military Nursing Service as a sister. She left in 1905, but returned to nursing in the Great War. She was awarded a Red Cross in 1916. Her sister Winnie Monck-Mason was a suffragette. Her great friend and cousin Jessie Street was a well known political activist in Australia.

In 1919 Edith eventually settled down and married Lt Colonel Harry Codrington, whose family were Indian Army through and through. She had wanted to marry him in her youth, but that was not possible for financial reasons. Sadly Harry Codrington's first wife was drowned when the SS *Persia* was torpedoed off Crete in 1915 and sank with great loss of life.

Below the Belt

This very moving story was only recently written down in August 2013 by the artist Saar Steenkamp née Grobler of Hantam near Namaqualand and was told to her by her grandmother. Some of these stories are only now coming out and it is very important that they are written down before they are lost. What this story also highlights is the division between the Boers after the war even within one family as to whether they were pro-British or anti-British. Their husbands may well have been caught at Brandwater Basin and sent abroad. Often I suspect it was the direct experience of the war rather than the overriding politics that influenced their choices. Many of the women left on the farms on their own were very brave and deeply resented seeing their farms burnt and their animals killed in front of their eyes. The story of the camps is a harrowing one.

Mounted soldiers, possibly New Zealanders, round up a Boer family

Emily Hobhouse

Increasingly the Boer War became very bitter indeed and the clearance of the farms and the civilian population was a publicity disaster in both humanitarian and political terms. The setting up of the camps was in fact intended as a relief measure, for the protection of the wives and children of the enemy, but it very soon became a living nightmare. Today the term 'concentration camp' is a very loaded one but it was a term used then to describe temporary tented accommodation for civilians in a war which they thought would be over by the autumn of 1900. The term 'internment camp' is more appropriate.

Emily Hobhouse did much to bring the world's attention to the plight of women and children who were forcibly kept in these camps. Kitchener hated her for it. He called her 'That Bloody Woman' but then again there was no way of telling whether he really liked any women at all.

Emily Hobhouse was born in Cornwall near Liskeard in 1860 and came from a liberal family. She nursed her mother for fourteen years then went off to Minnesota to help dry out the Cornish miners. She became engaged and then went to live on a ranch in Mexico. The engagement was eventually broken off and her money was in the end also lost. She was 'saved' by the Boer War and found a new mission in life.

Not all M.P.s were in favour of the war and one of them Leonard Courtenay, Penzance born and representing Liskeard and Bodmin, encouraged her to go to South Africa and report back to the South Africa Conciliation Committee. This committee was keen to get accurate information about the Boer War behind the

Malnutrition

scenes rather than the hyped up jingoistic press comments and the barrage of political rhetoric, which generally filled the papers everyday.

She was lucky to have a letter of introduction to Sir Alfred Milner himself and with the tacit approval of Kitchener she trundled off to Bloemfontein with two trucks and twelve tons of supplies. Back home she only knew of one camp and that was at Port Elizabeth. When she arrived Emily discovered that there were in fact thirty-four camps. One wonders what the other war correspondents were up to, and anyway they soon pushed off to the Boxer Rebellion in China or went home to write their own memoirs.

Emily was appalled at what she saw and wrote down her observations in letters which are stark and bleak. Many in England and in the government found them unpalatable. Her words, letters and reports however speak for themselves.

One of the main problems with the camps was the sheer scale of them and the lack of basic facilities. Disease soon took a hold and had a devastating effect on children. One acute problem in Bloemfontein was the fact that the Boers themselves had blown up the water treatment works which served the town. The actual numbers of deaths vary considerably. A rough estimate is that around 3,200 women died and about 23,000 children and 1,400 old men. Another problem was that the women did not necessarily trust the camp hospitals which were often understaffed and preferred to treat their children in their own tents with traditional remedies as they would have done on the farm. But they had no access to herbs or hygiene. Such rudimentary cures involved poultices made from cattle dung, which would

Water rations

only encourage infection. Malnutrition and an inadequate diet and a shortage of clean drinking water made things ten times worse.

The staff on the camps were not immune either. Between February 1901 and February 1902 the camps in the Transvaal lost forty-seven out of ninety-four doctors and eighty-five out of 217 nurses. Thirteen superintendents were replaced. If the camps were reasonably small and placed near good water then the survival rates were much higher.

The problem was the forced migration of people towards the camps. By 1901 relatively few families were displaced. It being regarded as a greater problem for the Boers to keep their families on the move, which would hinder a guerrilla war rather than help them. Towards the end of the war many Boers were glad that their families were in fact inside camps guarded by British soldiers, as the native community which was by now well armed, was getting very restless. Family groups often moved around like nomads, trying to keep away from the fighting just to stay alive. There were separate internment camps for blacks and no one really knows how many died there. Estimates vary between 10,000 to 20,000. Some would have been servants of the Boers.

Emily Hobhouse's reports were snapped up and published by the *Guardian*. This led to the Fawcett Commission under Dame Millicent Garrett Fawcett, who

A defiant Boer lady being evicted from her farm

had co-founded Newnham College, Cambridge.

Needless to say Emily Hobhouse was loved by the Boers and she is now regarded almost as a patron saint. She became life-long friends with the wife of President Steyn, who, realising that Emily was impoverished, managed to collect enough money so that Emily was able to buy a house in St Ives, Cornwall. This now forms part of Porthminster Hotel.

Mrs Otto Krantz. Her Husband Otto Krantz was in the German corps, which was part of the Vryheid-Commando that took part in the siege of Ladysmith. He was also at Elandslaagte and Tugela River. When he was captured Mrs Krantz went with him to captivity in Ceylon.

Not all camps were however badly run. Very slowly conditions did improve and so Emily Hobhouse's work was not in vain. Towards the end of the war there were for instance, two camps in Natal each housing 3,000 people. They were well organised and laid out like a town, with schools and hospitals. Apparently only forty-seven people died in Jacobs and seventeen in Wentworth. Keeping disease at bay was of fundamental importance.

Part 6

The Bitter End

Breaker Morant

'They don't shoot poets do they?'
Before Lorca's time my boy
And anyway I grant you
He wasn't 100% Aussie.
Born and raised in Somerset
Where the cider apples grow.

A pommy bastard true enough
With an Irish mother
But he made it down under
The Union in more senses than one.

But he was wild all right
Breaking horses and women's hearts
The outback got the better of him
Even Daisy Bates threw him out
For not paying his wedding bill
And stealing a few pigs.

But he got the better of Dargin's Grey
No easy matter breaking that one in.
But Daisy was a bit wild herself, being Irish
Took to writing like a duck to water.

He got on fine with Banjo Patterson
Waltzing Matilda and the sheep shearers' strike
But by then Daisy had her fill
And went native herself
But she had taught him a thing or two.
So of course when the Boer War came along
He waltzed off to South Africa
Signed on the dotted line
Went a bit wild for a year and half
Out on patrol, the Bushveldt Carbineers.

But things got tough toward the end:
Dog eat Dog – 'Take No Prisoners'
Straight from the horse's mouth –

Edwin Henry Murrant

'Bitter enders' and the fate of his best mate.
Went berserk more or less
Each farmhouse a shoot out —
And then if the Boers were wearing
British uniform that was Rule 303.

But word got back to base
He had exceeded orders,
And anyway the authorities
Were keen to appease the Boers
And keep the peace talks on track.

So he was court-martialled.
Pleaded guilty: 'Only following orders, Sir!'
But the orders somehow went missing
Like the transcripts of the trial.

Shot at dawn, after writing his last poem.
Bit unfair that. Refused a blindfold.

'Let us toss a bumper down our throat —
     Before we pass to Heaven
And toast the trim set petticoat
     We leave behind in Devon.'

'Shoot Straight you Bastards.'
     'Don't make a mess of it.'

Rooiwal

'I was just saying to the staff officer
That there were no Boers within twenty miles,
When we heard a roar of musketry
and saw a lot of men galloping down on us.'

'I never saw a more splendid attack.'
'They came on in one long line
Four deep and knee to knee.'
A good five hundred yards under direct fire

'Carbon copy of the Light Brigade, old boy'.
Suicidal and vastly outnumbered,
'They came on in one long line
Four deep and knee to knee'.

Picked off one by one, their General
In a blue shirt shot through the head,
A neatly trimmed beard, Potgieter himself
Only 30 yards from the front line.

'I never saw a more splendid attack.'
The Boers had taken the bait,
Forty Mounted Infantry on the skyline
Galloped up hill with slouch hats and carbines

Kept firing from the saddle
An unexpected ambush.
The red valley now redder than ever.

And when the line had turned we gave chase
Twenty miles. 'Tally Ho' as if it was the fox.
Complete waste of life
One young Boer boy lay there wounded
And in British uniform.

We let him off with a warning
Could have been shot you see –
Kitchener's orders were still in force
'Last scrap we ever had.'

Potgieter and his horse lying in front of the British line

Peace at Last

It was not the first time
The olive branch was proffered.
But the status of Cape Rebels
And the words 'Allegiance to the Crown'
Had stuck in the farmers' throats
Like barbed wire before breakfast.

They could not swallow the bait.

Anyway Sir Alfred was having none of it.
He had dreams of his own to fulfil.
His own bitter end was nothing short
Of overall control.

He wanted mastery of Africa:
Game, Set and Match.
But the tsetse fly eventually saw to that.

But Herbert, alias Kitchener of Khartoum,
To give credit where credit is due,
Wanted peace and he wanted it very badly.
He had wanted it for years.

The cavalcade of 'drives' and 'bags'
Was almost at an end.
Barbed wire and blockhouse
Was not war as he understood it.

Burning farms was not gentlemanly,
Not 'home counties'
And the long lines of bell tents
Were a political eyesore back home.
Thanks to that 'Bloody Woman'.

Anyway Kitchener wanted India
And he wanted India badly.

As it turned out Herbert got on
Very well with Jan Smuts,
Who had, after all, run rings
Around his troops, for years and years.

Between them they hatched
A little plan of their own.
A set of words
Which worked for both Republics.

Herbert's sidekick, Ian Hamilton,
Captured and wounded at Majuba,
A liberal linguist and a poet,
Was invited to attend a birthday party
For Smuts, just like old times…
After that the Boers were the 'Best men in Africa'

Secretly they admired each other.
The Boers had taught the British many new tricks
And brought them up to speed.
As if in a circus tent, with Kitchener as ring master.

Huffing and puffing. It just depended
Who was making the Lion jump through the hoop.

Hamilton also wrote a letter to his young friend
Warning Churchill about Milner's little plan
To prolong the war
And said that 'he now understood
Why the talks at Bloemfontein
Had failed three years before'
When Kruger dug Sir Alfred in the ribs as a joke.

The military were no fools.
Hardened in war but no fools.
They hated the way the war was going.

As it was they all signed
The Treaty of Vereeniging
In Pretoria as it happens
Just before midnight in Melrose House.

A small discrete scruffy looking
Four page typed document
Which amongst other things
Gave the Boers £3 million pounds.

The signatures are there
On the right hand side
Reitz, Botha, de la Rey, de Wet,
And half a dozen more including Burger,
And Hertzog just to make sure.

And on the left Kitchener of Khartoum
And Milner. Done and dusted Sir Alfred.
A war which should never really have started.

Back home Fredrick Pine Theophilus Struben
Was digging for tin on the edge
Of Dartmoor above the River Dart.

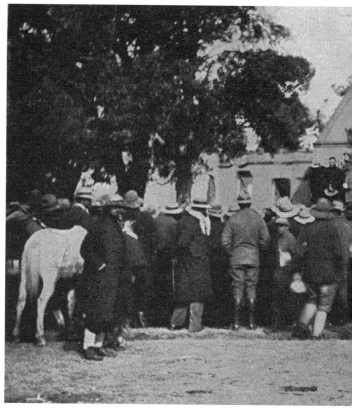

*Generals Elliot and De Wet explaining to Boer officers the conditions
of peace. Winburg Orange Free State*

And as for Kitchener he came unstuck
A few years later off the Orkneys
On his way to Archangel

Struck a mine... of another sort.

Horse Tally

Difficult to say exactly what the tally was, Sir
But we have worked out that on the British side at least, Sir
Over 400,000 horses, mules and donkeys
Were expended in the war effort, Sir

400,346 to be precise Sir - Nearly half a million, Sir.
Of that I should say 300,000 were horses.
50,000 came from the States, 35,000 from Australia, Canada
And New Zealand - an unknown quantity from the Argentine, S

Many remounts came into Port Elizabeth

For the Mounted Infantry. Only paid on average £8 for those
The others were more, Sir, some £12 other £16 for *walers*
The English cavalry horse if you remember was around £40, Sir
Very costly indeed, Sir. In round terms, Sir, £7 million.
Losses? If you remember French lost over five hundred

In a single day on his way to Kimberley, ridden to death
Over heated Sir. Carrying too much equipment.
Not enough water and grazing. No rest. Many were shot, Sir.
In Ladysmith, Sir, the 18th and 19th Hussars and Natal Carbineers
Had to eat their own horses, Sir. Made something called Chevril,
In the railway yards, rendered down. Not bad by all accounts.
Like beef tea. Very good in hospital, Sir. Saved many lives.

There is, Sir, some talk of putting up a memorial to the horses.
In Port Elizabeth. Funded by public subscription.
Ladies of the town, Sir, have formed a committee
A Mrs Harriet Meyer is President. It can't do any harm I thought.

It is a statue, Sir, a horse with its head bowed and a soldier
Kneeling down giving the horse a drink of water from a bucket, Sir.
Very touching. I have seen a sketch. My wife approves.
It will be cast in bronze I understand, with a granite plinth, Sir.

Midday break

The Human Tally

Human losses, Sir? Bit difficult to get exact figures.
You see we had over 450,000 in the field by the end of the war.

Not easy keeping track of them. Over 80,000 were colonials
They never liked keeping records. Very good soldiers. Bit unruly, Sir.

Lost a lot at the beginning Sir. If you remember.
About 22,000 died Sir in total. 5,784 killed in action

Plus another 2,100 who died of wounds
Another 13,250 are estimated to have died of disease.

Then again there were 934 missing, still not sure
What happened to them, Sir. Maybe they will turn up one day.

So that makes it just over 22,000. 22,068 to be precise.
And another 22,828 were wounded but made a recovery of sorts.

Disease, Sir ? Yes that was a bit of a problem. Mainly enteric fever
And malaria, dysentery, pneumonia. That sort of thing.

So on balance we lost almost three times the number of men
To disease than killed in action Sir. Bit unfortunate, Sir.

As to the enemy, Sir? even more difficult to say, Sir.
Records very scarce. They had about 88,000 in the field.

Of whom 2,000 were from overseas. Irish, German, Italian, Russian
French etc and about 13,000 Afrikaners from Cape Colony and Natal.

enemy casualties? Then again very difficult, often buried on the spot.
About 4,000 killed in action we estimate and another 5,000

Died of wounds or disease. Boer prisoners? That's a bit easier
Over 25,000 were sent overseas. St Helena, Ceylon, Bermuda and India.

As to the civilian camps Sir Again we are not really sure.
Some say 18,000 died mostly of disease - others that it is nearer 28,000

Mostly women and children. Very unfortunate, Sir
The black native population. No real idea. Maybe another 14,000 Sir.

Also, Sir, I thought you would like to know that over 8,000
Blockhouses were built and 3,700 miles of barbed wire fence.

Farmhouses, Sir? Officially 600, Sir, destroyed but certain reports
Put the figure much, much higher maybe 30,000, Sir

And up to 3.6 million sheep were destroyed.
The cattle we ate, Sir, if you remember, those had to feed the troops

It was a costly war, Sir. Very costly.
Let's hope we don't have another one like it ever again, Sir.

Ah the real cost of the war. Well Sir, that...
That was around £211 million pounds, Sir – with interest included.

Is that all, Sir?
Coffee?

Boer War Veteran

'Hellish good of you to come
and see an old buffer like me
Doing a desk job now…'

Jabs his finger at the wall
Uncle Theodore,
Ninety-one in the shade

Of a single light bulb
Black patch over one eye,
Grey whiskers and stubble

Lives alone, lives in his striped pyjamas
Sits in his bedsit
Unable to see the horizon

Rubs a dirty glass with an old
Handkerchief, his daily tipple
A stirrup cup of barley wine,

Raw egg and cheese.
At four in the morning
The veld still folded tightly around him

A blanket of stars, a pillow of tea
Been sleeping rough for months on end
His memories tethered for the night

Then saddled before dawn.
Khaki deceptive in the early light
The uniform approach

Wary of outriders looking like
Your own. Slouch hats
Ambush when you least expect it.

'Going to stale' he announces
In a voice that could be heard in Pretoria
Then staggers to the outside loo.

'Hellish good of you to come
And see an old buffer like me
Doing a desk job now … '

Five shillings a day and slouch hats
Swashbuckling load of bandits,
Wild bunch of cattle thieves

Number three held the horses
Soon got wise to that one
'Hit the Trail.' 'Hit the Trail.'

Trooper Theodore Fleming, Bethune's Mounted Infantry
Interviewed Bexhill-on-Sea, 5 November 1975

The Bitter End

Breaker Morant

The case of Edwin Henry Murrant, otherwise known as 'Breaker Morant', because of his ability to break wild horses is a curious and lamentable story. He was a Somerset lad born in 1864 and brought up in the Bridgwater Union which was run by his parents. His father died when he was only 4 months old and his mother Catherine Reilly had to bring him up on her own. No easy matter in a workhouse. But he was talented and by 1881 he was working as a tutor at Silesia College in North London.

Then he went to Australia and led a fairly wild life in the outback. Dargin's Grey was a notorious bucking bronco and Breaker managed to ride him successfully at the Bathurst Show.

Daisy Bates, Breaker's wife, ended up becoming one of Australia's pioneer anthropologists and spent much time with the aboriginals. She learnt their language, even wrote a dictionary and championed their cause. She was regarded as an expert and was in contact with Professor Radcliffe Brown at Cambridge who apparently later borrowed extensively from her work which led to a few ructions. Meantime 'The Breaker' as he called himself had also become a poet and had over fifty poems published in *The Bulletin*. He was friends with other bush poets including Henry Lawson, William Ogilvie and

Banjo Patterson, who wrote 'Waltzing Matilda' in 1895 after the shearers' strikes and barn burnings of the early 1890s.

When the Boer War started 'Breaker Morant', as he now styled himself, joined the South Australian Mounted Rifles and was for a while on the staff and allocated as dispatch rider for the *Daily Telegraph* war correspondent Bennet Burleigh, who was no stranger to wars. Although British, Burleigh had not only fought alongside Garibaldi in Sicily, he had fought in the American Civil War on the Confederate side. He had also had fought in the Sudan when his 'square' was broken. He was always critical of the army's weapons. I suspect Bennet Burleigh and Breaker Morant got on very well indeed, each having a bit of a wild streak.

After serving in South Africa, Morant had six months leave back in England, most of which was spent with his good friend Captain Hunt, either out hunting or chasing young ladies in North Devon. They both became engaged to a pair of sisters in Bideford. On his return to South Africa, Breaker joined the Bushveldt Carbineers and was increasingly in many conflicts during the vicious tail end of the guerrilla campaign. At one shoot out at Devils' Claw farmhouse defended by Field Cornet Viljoen, whom they had cornered, Captain Hunt was badly wounded and had to be left behind. Next day they found his dead body beaten up, stripped and mutilated.

Breaker 'saw red' and went all out to kill Boers even if they had surrendered. A few days later he ordered eight prisoners to be shot whom he believed had been involved in the killing of Captain Hunt. Some apparently had bits of Captain Hunt's clothing. A German missionary was also shot, possibly as a witness, but the circumstances were unclear. It later turned out that Captain Hunt's body had been mutilated by local tribesmen.

As it was any Boer found wearing British army uniform was also likely to be shot. So Breaker was in his own mind only following orders. Interestingly up till that point Captain Hunt and Morant did not shoot prisoners and were even reprimanded by their superiors for bringing prisoners in. Other units were also involved in shootings. It was a very murky war indeed towards the end and certainly not a 'Gentleman's War'. Furious that officers were becoming out of control and giving him a bad name, Kitchener ordered an investigation into the Bushveldt Carbineers. The men who had been ordered to do the shootings were becoming very uneasy, and not surprisingly, had begun to talk.

Breaker Morant was tried with two other officers, Lt Handcock and Lt Witton. They did not deny the charges. But the trial was far from perfect, evidence was suppressed and key witnesses were sent abroad. All the papers from the trial subsequently disappeared. Breaker wanted to put Kitchener in the witness box and cross examine him about his 'No Prisoners' order, which had apparently been in force for over year. In the end both Breaker and another officer Lt Handcock were found guilty and sentenced to be shot.

The execution was carried out on 27 February 1902. Lt Witton was given penal servitude and later wrote about his experiences. It is a case which still resonates today and has sparked much controversy, several books and at least one film which featured Edward Woodward.

Rooiwal

This was the last real battle to be fought during the Boer War. It took place on 11 April 1902 and unusual to say the least. It was also the last Boer cavalry charge. For days, weeks and months the Boer commandos and the British Forces played a game of cat and mouse. Blockhouses and barbed wire had taken their toll. Eventually the Boers who were against the idea of peace being signed decided to break out of the noose which was being drawn tighter and tighter round them. They charged at the British forces, foolishly almost like the Light Brigade. It was magnificent and over 1,500 men charged. The Boers were only stopped about thirty yards from the British line, General Potgieter being one of their dead. There were over 300 casualties, though there could easily have been a lot more. It was totally uncharacteristic of the Boers to charge, and was probably a sign of their deep frustration more than anything else. The other Boer General Jan Kemp survived. His grandfather was the stepson of Piet Retief. On the British

Hollander Korps at Zandspruit

side Robert Kekewich, a Devon man, was in charge. He had defended Kimberley and was helped by Ian Hamilton and Henry Rawlinson who had both been at the Siege of Ladysmith.

It was the end of the road. In just over a month both sides were talking to each other. By the end of May the ink was drying on the peace agreement. They had come a long way since the failed talks in Bloemfontein. Jan Kemp wanted to keep fighting and refused to sign.

Peace at Last

The peace negotiations were never easy. When Kitchener had advocated peace back in 1900 the good burghers who had taken the message back to the commandos like Meyer van Cock were executed by their own side as traitors. In March 1901 there was another attempt at peace negotiations at Middleburg. This also failed. After the attack at Rooiwal most Boers still fighting realised the game was up. The Zulus and other black tribesmen were turning against them, and were armed with rifles. The large number of atrocities committed by the Boers on captured black auxiliaries who worked for the British whether armed or not, did not help their cause. The Boers grudgingly accepted that their women and children were ironically safer in the British camps than out in the high veld. Nearly 6,000 Boers were 'joiners' fighting on the British side. The brutal scorched earth policy was taking its toll. Clothing was so scarce that Boers often had to resort wearing women's clothing or captured British uniforms which made them liable to be shot. The longer they continued fighting, the more draconian the peace would be. In the end it was a political decision which Smuts engineered with Kitchener under the noses of Sir Alfred Milner and Dr Steyn.

It was a bitter blow but it was a common sense, pragmatic decision. Everyone was fed up with a guerrilla war which had degenerated into brutality. Ironically the peace was signed on 31 May 1902 exactly three years since the beginning of the Bloemfontein talks, which had been scuppered by Milner. Both Ian Hamilton and Kitchener had rumbled this and did not want Milner to scupper their chances again.

As it happened Ian Hamilton, as with many British officers had great respect for the Boer leaders because of their skill at fighting a running guerrilla war. Hamilton was a poet and novelist, and unusually intelligent for a British general. He spoke French, German and Hindi and was a Liberal. He later opposed conscription. His wars had started in 1878 with the Second Afghan War and he died in 1947, two years after the Second World War had ended.

Africa got its revenge on Sir Alfred Milner in the end, who, in 1925 was sadly bitten by a tsetse fly and later died of sleeping sickness. His kindergarten of colonial administrators was famous. One of his best known protégés was John Buchan, the novelist who wrote *Greenmantle* and *Prester John*.

Kitchener was drowned when his ship the cruiser, *HMS Hampshire* was sunk by a mine off Orkney in June 1916. He was on his way to Archangel, in North Russia. Several dissident groups claimed the credit for sinking *HMS Hampshire* and killing Kitchener, including Irish Rebels, Russian communist elements, who had betrayed the route of the ships to the Germans, and even more bizarrely the Boers. Frederick Joubert Duquesne, Piet

Joubert's nephew reared his head once again. He had apparently tried to assassinate Kitchener in Cape Town. Then in 1916 he allegedly posed as the Russian Duke, Boris Zakrevsky, and joined Kitchener in Scotland. Then when on board *HMS Hampshire*, signalled the U boat which was waiting for him. The U boat torpedoed the ship and Duquesne escaped in a raft and lived happily ever after with an Iron Cross pinned to his chest. None of these alternative versions were of course ever proven or taken seriously. The accepted version is that *HMS Hampshire* struck a mine laid by U 75. There were also rumours of gold bullion destined to shore up the failing Russian Tsar. Even to this day no diving is allowed over the wreck.

During the First World War many Boers fought side by side with the British. Jan Smuts fought the Germans in South-West Africa and East Africa. He later became a Field Marshal in the British army, an unusual honour for a former adversary. His statue stands in Parliament Square, London cast in bronze by Jacob Epstein.

In a strange twist of fate, in 1940, there was a plan afoot recorded by Churchill's secretary, Sir John Colville, that should Churchill die or otherwise become incapacitated during the war, Smuts would then become Prime Minister of the United Kingdom. It had the backing of Queen Mary and George VI. What Parliament and the British people would have thought is another matter.

'That Bloody Woman' is of course Emily Hobhouse, who counted among her friends Mahatma Gandhi, who served as a stretcher bearer during the Boer War. The Boer War was at an end. But what they had actually been fighting for was still a bit of a mystery to most of the soldiers and even many people back home.

Horse Tally

The statue of the horse was eventually erected in 1905. The horse stands 16 hands 2 inches high. It cost around £2,500. The memorial was designed by Joseph Whitehead and cast in bronze by Thomas Dillon Works in Surrey.

It was unveiled on 11 February 1905 by the Mayor of Port Elizabeth Mr Alexander Fettes. The project was not without its difficulties and this was alluded to in part by the mayor's opening speech:

'The unveiling of this monument marks the completion of what has been an arduous undertaking on the part of those ladies with whom the idea of raising a monument to the horses originated.'

Port Elizabeth was where most of the horses were brought ashore from transport ships. Often under slung with a canvas sling and then craned out over the side to the quay. Many were remounts for the vast number of Mounted Infantry. The average life expectancy of a British horse from the time of its arrival in Port Elizabeth, was around six weeks. Sadly 60% of the horses died in combat or as the result of mistreatment. Of half the million or so horses used in the war around 350,000 died – 67% – and that was just on the British side.

Walers are Australian horses which were originally bred in New South Wales and were ideally suited for Mounted Infantry. The Walers carried the rider, saddle, saddle cloth, bridle, head collar, lead rope, a horseshoe case with one front and one hind shoe, nails, rations for the horse and rider, a bedroll, change of clothing, a rifle and about ninety rounds of .303 rifle ammunition.

Human Tally

The human cost of the war was enormous on both sides and the deaths of so many women and children in camps was unforgivable. Irreparable damage was done to a young country and Britain's reputation.

The financial cost of the war was also astronomic, and has been calculated to have been around £211 million which was about £6.6 million per month, in other words nearly £220,000 a day. Quite a staggering amount for those days. The breakdown of the financial cost of the war shows how the money was spent:

Supplies	£47,600,000
Ships and transport	£30,500,000
Other stores	£17,470,000
Horses, mules & oxen	£16,525,000
Railway costs	£15,700,000
Pay for regular forces	£14,500,000
Clothing	£9,400,000
Wages for transportation staff	£7,670,000
Pay for South African forces	£7,500,000
Pay for Imperial Yeomanry	£5,150,000
Works, telegraph and engineering works	£4,700,000
Compensation	£4,580,000
Ammunition	£4,315,000
Pay for Militia	£4,000,000
Concentration camp maintenance	£3,540,000
Gratuities for troops	£3,500,000

Pay for overseas colonials	£2,700,000
Pay for medical establishments	£2,270,000
Pensions (to 31 Mar 03)	£1,660,000
Miscellaneous costs	£1,270,000

When Cecil Rhodes died in March 1902 he was one of the wealthiest men in the world and he left around £6 million which to this day helps fund students to study at Oxford University. These are known as Rhodes Scholarships. Interestingly £6 million would have only paid for about one month of the Boer War.

Mark Twain was not that impressed with Cecil Rhodes. 'I admire him, I frankly confess it; and when his time comes I shall buy a piece of the rope for a keepsake'. As for Alfred Beit he also left large sums of money to various universities including Oxford, Hamburg and Imperial College.

The real cost of the war in terms of human suffering was of course incalculable. If only they had come to a sensible agreement in Bloemfontein in early June 1899. Bloemfontein was also the birthplace of J.R.R. Tolkien. There are still avenues of jacaranda trees there today.

Boer War Veteran

Trooper Theodore Vandermere Fleming was in fact my great, great uncle and I was lucky enough to be able to interview him in 1975 in Bexhill-on-Sea. And it is from this meeting that my interest in the Boer War stems. I myself was in the army at the time and it was fascinating to hear his stories first hand. Only later did I discover that another uncle had served in the 2nd Scottish Horse called James Scott Crowden and he had been at Bakenlaagte when Colonel Benson was killed.

As with many young men Theodore Fleming ran away to the Boer War when he was seventeen and worked with Remounts before joining Bethune's Mounted Infantry. His impressions of the Boers, his respect for them as soldiers and the dangers of patrolling, stayed with me ever since.

After the Boer War he legged it to the Yukon and became a constable in the North-West Mounted Police in Whitehorse. A Mountie in other words. Hence his parting words 'Hit the Trail'. They often did three week dog sledge patrols in arctic conditions. So from one extreme of climate to another. One of his very good friends out there was a young bank manager called Robert Service who later became a very well known Canadian poet. Uncle Theodore apparently led Robert Service astray and not only took him down the red light district but also took him back to the N.W.M.P. canteen where he would have heard all their stories when coming off patrol, which he then turned into poetry. Uncle Theodore ate mammoth, eventually came back to England and then married Gertrude. He served in the First War and won an M.C. in Italy for bringing mules out under fire. In the Second War he was C.O. of a prison of war camp near Royston in Hertfordshire.

His eldest brother Edward Fleming won a gold medal for poetry at Cambridge, stayed safely at home but worked in the War Office and was responsible for 'Manning'. During the First War it was across his desk that all the casualty lists went every day, every name of every soldier killed, missing, captured, or presumed dead. Kitchener's little army chewed up and spat out.

Later he became very involved in the War Graves commission. He could even see the Cenotaph from his pepper pot office on the top floor of the Old War Office.

Theodore Fleming's memories however of the Boer War were crystal clear and never left him. It was the sight of the Boer commando surrendering which moved him most, that, and the nurses on the troop train. His middle name was Vandermere which of course is Dutch Flemish and he was Irish as well.

Theodore died in Bexhill-on-Sea a year later in 1976 aged 92. He was apparently regaling the local nurses with his tales of the Boer War and Yukon right till the very end, even daring to pinch their bottoms from time to time. No doubt they responded in kind. He wanted his ashes thrown off Beachy Head with the hunting horn playing 'Gone Away'.

Children going to get water

Al Fresco lunch – Officers' Mess – 1st Coldstream Guards

'Basuto Boys' before going out on night patrol along the railway line near Thebus. Note blockhouse in the background.

Longueville
Diaries

LONGUEVILLE DIARIES

Just as this book was about to go to print, I discovered the existence of these excellent diaries and was able to have a good read of them: all thanks to my local acupuncturist, Rosemary Norton. She was sticking needles into me one day and she casually mentioned that her grandfather, Reginald Longueville had been in the Boer War, as had her great uncle Edward. She went back to have a look at the diaries and yes, such names as Modder River and Magersfontein did indeed appear in the margins. There were three volumes handwritten and two volumes of photographs. He had been right in the thick of it. He was a Captain in 1st Battalion Coldstream Guards commanding 6 Company and his brother Edward a Lieutenant in the 2nd Battalion.

The style of the diaries was just what I wanted, the true language of war, but very laid back almost like a country parson observing the habits of his parishioners.

Reginald Longueville with pet baboon

Very down to earth and practical. Just straightforward, good accurate observation. He was also a master of understatement and very self deprecating. He has great compassion for the common soldier and even the Boers, from time to time, particularly when searching their houses for weapons. The 'poetry' is in his honesty and attention to detail.

Even on the very first page, almost by way of apology, he observes that this is: *'A rough day to day diary from October 1899 – August 1902 compiled from old pocket diaries and letters'* and underneath in a small pencil jotting, barely legible, he says *'Not worth the trouble of reading, much less correcting style, English, the spelling. In fact not worth reading at all'.*

Captain Reginald Longueville
1st Coldstream Guards
near Pretoria June 1900

In fact they are an extraordinarily rich resource and tell me far more about the battles than official regimental war histories and the jingoistic jargon of some war correspondents. He must have been incredibly brave and if he had not survived the Boer War, my acupuncturist would not be here today, working at the sharp end.

Sadly I can only include a few excerpts but I have, I hope, picked up some of the key moments. Reginald Longueville was born in 1869 so he was 30 when the Boer War started and had been in the army long enough to know its little ways. He came from around Oswestry and could, if he wanted to, trace his ancestry right back to 1066 and the Norman knights. One of his ancestors in 1799 was killed in a duel with his guardian!

The diary starts in Gibraltar where they are about to embark for Cape Town. Luckily Reginald Longueville also took a camera with him and has left at least two volumes of photographs, some of which are reproduced here.

Gibraltar

We and the 3rd Grenadier Guards
Were inspected by the Governor –
Sir Robert Biddulph. Marched past etc.

He told us we would probably have
'A lot of marching but probably not much fighting'.
A beastly *Levanter* on today.

Took a room at the Bristol Hotel
Buying every sort of thing for active service
Some Chlorydyne, a tourniquet to carry in my pocket

Some small hair brushes...
Our ship detained by fog but it is on its way
3rd Grenadiers embarked on *The Ghoorkha*

I saw them off. Packed my valise
Which is allowed to weigh 35 lbs
Sent a telegram home to say 'Goodbye'.

Paraded after luncheon and embarked on
P&0 *SS Malta*. Leave takings and bands
'Girl I left Behind' etc.

And we steamed away at about 6.30 p.m.
HMS Anson was in harbour; and as we passed
They 'cheered ship' which sounded awfully well.

I am in a very good cabin,
Just off midships on the starboard side.
Geoffrey Fielding is with me.

23-28 October 1899

P and O. S.S. *Malta*
Off Berbera.
Had a lumpy passage so far, both over...

Life on the Ocean Wave

Colonel Codrington, who was always busy,
Spent a good deal of time in sharpening
His sword with a small oil stone.

I gave mine to the ship's butcher
Who put such an edge on it that it was
A most dangerous weapon even to its owner.

The men had rifle practice at some targets
We towed behind the ship. The officers had some
Revolver practice and did not have an accident!

We came into a very heavy head sea,
Our ship behaved beautifully
And is a capital sea boat.

I did not suffer from 'Mal de Mer'.
We passed the mail boat going home
But too far off to signal and ask for news.

We could only see the lights
And that she had a good roll on,
So I filled my old flask with whisky.

November 1899

Medical Matters

The Medical Officer, Crooke-Lawless,
And his assistant then produced their implements
For inoculation against enteric.

It is not a pleasant process as it gives
One an awful 'head' and makes
One feel very wretched for 24 hours.

Crooke-Lawless also gave us all
A lecture on first aid to the wounded
And how to use a field dressing.

In order to show the position
Of the arteries he marked them upon
His servant in 'indelible ink pencil'

The man must have had a nice business
To get the marks off again.
We all had to be passed by the doctors

As to our fitness for active service.
The poor doctor was very tired.
He put his stethoscope

On my Field Pocket Book
Which was in my breast pocket.
I don't think he would have heard much through it.

November 1899

The Briefing

We arrived at Cape Town early.
A staff officer came on board
And we were very eager for news.

It was the opinion of many of us
That the war would be all over
By the time we got there

And we had heard nothing for so long.
All his news seemed bad news
Of disasters and defeats or something very like it.

16 November 1899

Movement Orders

We disembarked about 2 p.m.
The right half battalion left by train

About 4 p.m. and the second half,
Including my company, left at 8.40 p.m.

The officers were in first class carriages
And the men in second and third.

At daylight we were in 'Hex Valley'
Very fine mountain scenery.

We stopped for breakfast
At a small station and later

For other meals which we got
Very comfortably in refreshment rooms.

17 November 1899

Daily orders and mail South African Light Horse

Touching Base

Reached De Aar, a small village of tin houses
A good many troops and lots of stores.
It seemed to me all dust and brilliant sunshine.

Saw General Wauchope (soon afterwards
Killed at Magersfontein) on the platform
A very striking looking man.

We were told that the enemy
Were to the north-east and that we
Should possibly be shot at en-route.

We arrived at Orange River Station at about 5 p.m.
The rest of the Guards Brigade are near there.
I saw Edward, my brother, who is transport officer

Of the 2nd Battalion, looking very fit and well
With a very promising crop of beard and whiskers.
He had bought a very nice cream coloured Boer pony.

Edward Longueville with his Boer pony

We are encamped in tents. We had our first experience
Of South African dust which blew in clouds.
A bright blue sky, a glaring sun and any amount of dust.

Teams of mules and drivers,
Artillery horses going to water and
Crowds of soldiers with very sunburnt faces

Unloading baggage and stacking it up.
Kimberley is being besieged by the Boers
And we are going to relieve it.

18 November 1899

War Paint

We have two batteries Royal Artillery here
75th & 18th Field Batteries

An easy day in camp
In order to avoid all glitter

And to avoid betraying ourselves
By bright buttons etc., we painted our buttons

And all shining things with khaki paint
We started a coffee bar as we had a few stores.

20 November 1899

Belmont 1

We entrained about 4 p.m. in trucks
And went to WITTEPUTS
A small siding a few miles up the line
Detrained there and started to march.

Just at dusk we halted and meant to have tea.
Message came from Lord Methuen
That he was going to attack the enemy at dawn,
So we decided to push on and be in time if possible.

We moved off in fours. The companies in front
Moved off very fast and we had some difficulty
Keeping in touch as it was by this time
Very dark and we could not see the track.

We had a long march in the dark of about twelve miles
And at last reached the bivouac to the west
Of the fence at Thomas's Farm.
There were fires lit and the men were round them.

The Grenadiers very kindly gave us
Coffee and supper.
I remember talking to John Fryer
Who was killed early next day.

22 November 1899

Belmont 2

We woke our men soon after 1 a.m.
The fires had all gone out and it was
Very dark, stars were shining and it was cold.

Two companies: No. 6 and No. 3
Under my command were told off to guard
The stores and bivouacs from any flank attacks.

As I could not see the ground I had no idea
As to its form, but had to make
The best dispositions I could in the dark.

In looking round I found a house and saw Lord Methuen
Who told me to 'look out for a flank attack'.
The rest of the brigade marched away.

Lieutenant-General Lord Methuen

Just at dawn the firing began. We were close
Above the bivouac on some ridges by this time.
During the night some stores had arrived

And I got some 'Bully Beef and biscuits'
For my men and a man gave me a tin of coffee
Which I was very grateful of.

At about 11.30 or 12 noon I got orders
To take on the two companies
As a pick-up and burying party.

I marched them in till I met Colonel Mainwaring,
On the staff, who detailed to each company a portion
Of the battle field to search for dead and wounded.

A few Coldstreams with the latest transport to get supplies for the officers' mess from the nearest store

We got back at about 4 or 5 or 6 p.m.?
I cannot remember. I was very tired indeed
And was soon asleep. The British dead

Were brought back in wagons and buried
Near the bivouac that evening.
I did not go to the funeral being too sleepy.

23 November 1900

Belts and Braces

We were told to wear men's equipments
In order to make ourselves less conspicuous.
The belts and braces of the killed and wounded

Were collected and we fitted ourselves out.
I had a bath in a small stream. We rested all day.
In the evening about 4.30 p.m. we marched in rearguard.

Just at dusk there were supposed to be some Boers
In our rear, and during a halt we were ordered to make
Some small entrenchments, but no Boers appeared.

24 November 1899

Good Practice

We halted again near Graspan siding
The men had had nothing since early morning
And the sun was very hot and everybody

Was very thirsty. The more prudent people
Had left a little water in their water bottles.
But on being told 'officially' that we were to halt there

And cook dinners and that we should get water
From a tank there was by the railway,
Most people drank all their water.

We were soon told afterwards that all the water
In the tank was required for the wounded.
And that we were to march on at once.

We then had a march of six or seven miles.
We were all, awfully thirsty, the road was dusty
And the sun, very hot, our tongues were all dry

And our lips cracking and the men very tired.
Private Fowler, I remember said
"Cheer up lads this is good practice for 'ell".

After the Battle of Graspan Saturday 25 November 1899

Modder River 1

I remember seeing Colonel Stopford
At the head of the 2nd Battalion.
He was one of the first to be killed next day.
We bivouacked near the dam.

I had a delightful swim and bath having
Borrowed a towel and some soap from Edward.
We found a nice small spring of good water
Which was an immense luxury.

It was a very nice bivouac. And we were told
That we would probably stay here tomorrow
And looking forward to a long 'lie in'
In the morning, had ordered our breakfast at 7 a.m.

At dawn Ruggles Bryce, Grenadier Guards, Brigade Major
Woke me to ask where Colonel Codrington was sleeping.
I was awfully sleepy. We found him and Ruggles said...
'We were to march at once.' This was about 4 a.m.

We got some coffee and biscuits and some jam and started.
It was a nice morning. After about five miles we were halted
And a line of trees, where there was a village, was pointed
Out to us and we were told that it was believed

That it was held by the enemy, but not for an absolute
Certainty. We were to attack the village
And some tall poplar trees in the centre of it
Were to be the object of attack. My battalion were in support.

Modder River 2

Soon after we had deployed, firing had begun.
A shell went over my head and I was not sure
If it was one of ours, then another came and pitched
In front of us throwing up about a cartload of sand

And another passed over us and burst by a wagon.
So there was no doubt they were not ours!!
I had my company extended in echelon of half companies.
The ground was rather undulating.

We advanced and then near a ruined house,
Or kraal a shell burst in it and there was
A great blow up and I remember an old biscuit tin flying
A height into the air – we then came under rifle fire

Modder River

And a fair number of bullets hit up the sand around us,
But no one was hit. We then came upon a river flowing
Between steep banks rather like the Severn at Pentreheylin.
I found two companies there: Colonel Codrington and Fielding

Were trying to cross. Asked the Colonel if I should bring
My company across too, but he told me to go up the river.
Neither Colonel Codrington or Fielding were able to get across.
The river was the Reit. We went on and found the Scots Guards

Or some companies of them. I don't know how many.
We passed a dead horse. It was Colonel Paget's
And then I found No. 7 Company in front of me
And we halted there. Very heavy firing was going on.

A sniper was in some bushes on the far side of the river.
Who we could not locate. However No. 7 found his position
And he stopped his fire. We lay down on the bank of the river,
A few bullets came from the left and some from the right.

A machine gun of some sort got our range from a small house
On our right for about half a minute. The bullets stirred
The ground close in front of my face, and another just missed
My legs, and another hit Private Fowler in the heel,

Who was just behind me. They struck me as coming very hard.
We made what entrenchments we could with 'Wallace Spades'
And lay there all day. My Colour Sergeant Clifford
Had a narrow escape of a bad wound, a bullet grazed his arm

Making a weal along it as if he had been struck with a whip.
And another man had the hand guard shot off his rifle.
No. 7 Company in front of me could not advance further,
So there we stayed, we were very hot, as the sun was very powerful,

Very hungry and very thirsty, but we could get water
From the river, though at some risk. It was very thick
And muddy, like coffee. But excellent under
The circumstances. Incessant heavy firing went on all day.

The Boers had a Vickers machine gun
Which they fire repeatedly, a pom-pom,
Three shots in quick succession. This gun sounded
Very loud and had a particularly disagreeable report.

Modder River 3

Some Boers rode up towards us on our right
And were fired on and retired.
Then one with a white band on his arm
Came within 1,000 yards.

I thought he was a doctor
So would not let my men fire on him.
He came nearer and some shots were fired
And he retired towards Jacobsdal.

We had no maps except
The 'Tourist Map of South Africa',
Which being on a large scale
Was not much use for small operations.

Modder River 4

About 5 p.m. were told that at dusk
We would rush the enemies position with the bayonet
And that the signal would be a blue flare.
We waited but soon after dark we got orders

To retire as quietly as possible into an empty reservoir
About half a mile in the rear. We started in file.
I heard a great rattling and found that one man
Had some loose rounds of ammunition in his mess tin.

These were soon removed. We got to the reservoir.
My Colour Sergeant I think it was told me
That he nearly tumbled over a dead man on a stretcher.
And just after dark I came upon rows and rows

Of men lying in the reservoir. I thought
'By Jove we must have had a lot of casualties today'.
But they were only a battalion asleep.
We formed up in the reservoir and the men lay down.

The graves of Col Stopford and the Marquess of Winchester
Modder River

I found Gleichen lying on a stretcher, he had been shot
In the neck. We opened our emergency rations
And ate them. I found Winchester and some fellows
In the 2nd Battalion eating theirs.

We were told we were to advance early in the morning.
Surgeon Captain Thomas of the Scots Guards
Came across and had some food with us.
He had plenty of blood about him.

28 November 1899

Suppertime

Fife and drums at Thebus

Rest and Recuperation

A nice bathe in the river –
The Highlanders, from lying in the sun
On the day of the battle,
Have all got their legs in blisters
And many have bandages on.

We know nothing of what is going on
But there is a rumour that there will be
A big fight next Wednesday or Thursday.

We had some hard work unloading stores
From trains as they are very heavy
And the dust and heat is very bad.

We are very short of matches.

2 December 1899

Magersfontein 1

The enemy's position was heavily bombarded.
We struck our camp and packed our tents about 4.30 p.m.
Thus giving the enemy a good hint that we were coming!

Had some tea and waited till dusk and then we marched.
We crossed the drift and after we had gone about a mile or so,
Halted and lay down. It was a very dark night.

We started again at about 1 a.m. and moved on in quarter column.
It began to pour with rain and thunder and lightning.
We had the greatest difficulty in keeping our formation

And our direction, owing to the intense darkness,
The blinding rain, and the bushes and clumps of boulders
That broke our ranks as we advanced.
Once we lost touch with the battalion in front.
Our line of advance was along a telegraph wire.
The posts were thin and a long way apart

5 inch cow gun on the move

But man on a horse just touched the wire with a stick
So that helped to guide us.
We marched in absolute silence.

Magersfontein 2

We marched till just before dawn when we halted.
Just as day broke I saw we were in rather undulating ground
And suddenly on our left I heard what sounded

Like any amount of wagons galloping over rocks.
The sound was so intense that I hardly thought it was rifle fire,
But it was the Boers firing upon the Highland Brigade.

There was a ridge in front of us covered with small dark bushes
And we were told we were to attack it. We moved off at once
Nos. 4. 3. 2. 1. Companies in the front line.

Nos. 5 & 6 in echelon in support of the right and Nos. 7 & 8 in rear.
The ground was covered with clumps of thick bushes
After we had advanced some short distance I was ordered

To form to the right and to look out for an attack from that direction
I met a dismounted lancer coming from the right who said
In a very Scotch accent 'Ma Harrrse has been shot. What will I do?'
And one highlander turned up from somewhere
Who said that the General and most
Of the Highland Brigade had been killed.

December 1899

the greatest difficulties in keeping our formation and our direction owing to the intense darkness, the blinding rain, and the bush and clumps of boulders that broke our ranks as we advanced. Here we lost touch with the battalion in front; our line of advance was along a telegraph line, the posts were then an a long way apart; but a man on a horse could just reach the wire with a stick so that helped to guide us. We marched in absolute silence — We marched till just before dawn when we halted. Just as day broke I saw we were on rather undulating ground and suddenly on our left I heard what seemed like any amount of waggons galloping over rocks. The sound was so intense that I hardly thought it was rifle fire but it was the Boers firing upon the Highland Brigade. There was a ridge in front of us covered with small dark bushes and we were told we were to attack it. We moved off at once. nos. 4.3.2.1. Companies in the front line. no 5 and 6 in echelon in support of the right and no 7 and 8 in rear. The ground was covered with clumps of thick bushes. After we had advanced some short distance I was ordered to form to the right and look out for an attack from that direction. I met a dismounted lancer coming from the right who said in a very scotch accent "Ma Harse has been shot what will I do"? and a Highlander turned up from somewhere who said that the General and apparently most of the Highland Brigade had been killed. We could not see very far owing to the clumps of bushes.

Page from Captain Longueville's diary describing the Battle of Magersfontein 11 December 1899

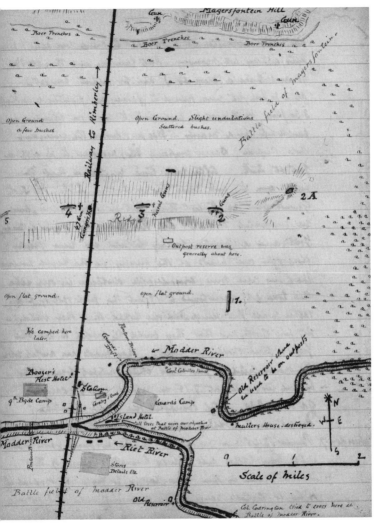

Captain Longueville's excellent sketch map of Modder River and Magersfontein battle fields

Magersfontein 3

We could not see very far owing to the clumps of bushes.
Ruggles Bryce, Brigade Major, came past and I asked him
If we had better advance or not. And he told me to stay where I w

There was heavy firing going on ahead in various parts of the batt
And some companies of the battalion caught it pretty hot.
We were ordered to make small entrenchments.

Heneage with a company of Grenadiers came and took up
A position on my right. It was very hot and we were very thirsty.
I had taken the precaution of filling a bottle of water

Besides my waterbottle and was very glad of a piece of cheese
I had saved from my last meal. In the afternoon
I was ordered to go and make a small fort on a little hillock

Covered in bushes about half a mile to my right.
I went there to look at the place and the enemy fired at me
With a pom-pom. The shells fell pretty close but did not hit me.

A small party of cavalry cantered past and they fired at them.
The shells burst right amongst their horses feet
And other's close to them but seemed to do no damage.

It soon began to get dark. Some of the companies retired
To the trench we had made and I took my company
To the little hill where we had made a small fort.

After dark a supply wagon came up and we got some
Bully beef biscuits and some rum which we were jolly glad of.
Here we spent the night which was a very cold one.

Monday 11 December 1899

Lucky Escape

We have two sentries; one specially
To keep an eye on Magersfontein Hill
So that when the Boers fire their gun
He can shout 'shell'
And give us timely warning
To squat down in the trench.

In the course of the morning
A cavalry Lieutenant with a small patrol
Came up to the fort. There is a gully
Up which one can come pretty close
Under cover from the enemy.

He asked me if he should go and explore
Some bushes about a mile away
To the South East. I told him to please himself
And that I did not want him to go on my account.
He went; and when they got nearer to the bushes
Some Boers who were concealed there fired on them
At pretty close range, and they came galloping back,

Straight at the fort so I could not fire for fear of
Shooting them. I saw the Boer bullets striking
Up the sand all around them but none of them were hit.

Wednesday 17 January 1900

Magersfontein from an outpost at the Modder River

Boers manning a shallow trench

Snipers

Some time afterwards Lord Methuen came up.
I ran out and warned him and his staff that there was sniping
Going on, so they left their horses in the gully.

One or two bullets came from snipers in the bushes
At last with my glasses I made out two Boers
Under a bush about 2,000 - 2,300 yards away

But I could not see them without the glasses
And as there were so many bushes it was very difficult
To explain which bush to my men.
I got one section and they fired a volley at the bush.

Some bullets fell very short; but, with my glasses,
I saw one or two hit just in front of the two Boers
Who got up and disappeared. The sniping then stopped.

Wednesday 17 January 1900

Blindfolded Messengers from the Boers –
General Reginald Pole-Carew considering his response.
In attendance, Lt Francis Farquhar, Captain Hughes, Major Stanley
Maude and General Inigo Jones..

Tarantula

Edward caught a Tarantula spider
A Most savage beast.
It had a great fight with a scorpion of mine.

The Scorpion stung him
And he collapsed;
But recovered some hours later.

24 January 1900

Scorpion

Stood to arms for an hour before dawn
And then back to base camp.
There are plenty of millipedes on the veldt
They are a sort of centipede,
Black with yellow legs
Of which there are thousands

They move very slowly
Are about 6 to 9 inches long
And about as thick as a thin walking stick
And have a sort of hard shell like covering.
They are nasty biters; but I believe are harmless.

Then there is the centipede an awful brute
About 4 to 7 inches long, flat, red,
With legs all long each side.
Very quick and active which bites and stings.

I caught one yesterday and put him
In a tin with a large scorpion.

He took no notice of the scorpion
Till the latter touched him, when suddenly
He instantly curled himself round the scorpion
Like a muscle, holding on with all his legs
And so holding the scorpion's tail
That he could not sting him,
Bit deep into the scorpion
With his horrid mouth and ate him!

It was such a horrid and unexpected performance
That it made me feel quite creepy.

Friday 26 January 1900

Chocolate

We have all got a box of chocolate
From H.M. Queen Victoria.
So many men have posted their boxes home
That the Post Office men say
That there is no room for more this mail.

I have just been handed £120 in gold
And £50 in half crowns. Canteen Money.
I have nowhere to lock it up.
Being Canteen President is a bit of a nuisance.

The men get a pint of beer each day now.
But are made to drink it there and then,
Otherwise they would probably sell it to each other
And then some would be drunk.

There is signalling by flash light
To Kimberley every night.
I wonder when it will be relieved?

Saturday 27 January 1900

Klip Drift

We then marched all night about nineteen miles, the last few
Of which were very tiring and then reached Klip Drift
We found a good many dead horses the last mile or so

Which were very 'strong'. We crossed the drift
And a short way beyond piled arms.
We had no transport and are in 'light order'.

No greatcoats or blankets and are on 'half rations'
And not much of them. We got some coffee and biscuits
About 7 a.m. and some 'mutton' – a sort of old goat.

Very tough and we had no salt.
Some tea and a ration of rum about 5 p.m.
Had a nice bathe in the river, then outposts for the night.

There is a charming simplicity about going to bed
As we have no greatcoats or blankets. It was pretty cold
During the night – of course we had no tents.

19 February 1900

Captain Reginald Longueville

Last Supper

The surroundings of the camp were horrible
There are dead horses and dead oxen
And there had been a Boer encampment here.

Apparently their practice is to kill a lot of sheep
So many men to a sheep. Killed all over the place
Just those parts they wanted eaten and the rest,

Insides etc. just left on the ground.
So the place is far from sweet. We are burying them
By degrees but one is always finding fresh horses.

Transport has not come yet, so no coats or blankets
I got an old piece of canvas from an abandoned
Boer wagon. So am all right for the night.

20 February 1900

We found a lot of buried Boer ammunition
Shells and rifle cartridges.
They were thrown in the river.
The men bathe in the river
And are always fishing them out again.

23 February 1900

We have made a bridge across the river
By putting some of the Boer wagons across it.
The river has risen after the rain
And dead animals come floating down.

Smell of dead horse very unpleasant!

Sunday 15 February 1900

Médecins Sans Frontières

A Boer doctor, a German I think,
Drove up in the dark, and asked my sentry
For a courtesy pass as he wished to go through
The lines and join the Boers somewhere.

He had come from Jacobsdal and in the course
Of the conversation he told me we should never
Be able to cross the Vaal river
As Boers would take up an impregnable position there.

He said 'The Boers must win in the end'
I said 'We would see in time' and he said 'We would'.
I sent him into headquarters.
We heard heavy gun fire in the east.

26 February 1900

En Passage

All the Boer prisoners from Paardeberg
Passed and halted here.
There are a tremendous lot of them

They are a very unkempt looking crew
All in plain clothes, old men, young men
Every sort of fellow.
They carry their belongings in blankets.
Many have them rolled with rug straps
And many have umbrellas.

We went and talked to them
Most of them could speak English
In a sort of way – some very well.
One man told me he was a photographer
From Johannesburg. He said he was very glad
That the war was over as far as he was concerned.

Bell tents

Major Albrecht

I saw Major Albrecht who commanded their guns
At Magersfontein. A fine looking fellow
Who had been in the German army.

Some of the commandants were mounted
And some old fellows and men who could not walk
Were in wagons. They all said they hated walking.

There was a very striking old boy – a commandant
On a pony with a billycock hat and an umbrella
Wolmarans I think his name was.

We got some flour that the Boers had left behind
And Drummond Hay made some cakes, but we had
No baking powder. They were not much of a success.

1 March 1900

Fever

Feel beastly. That is the only way of expressing it
Could not eat and feel quite dizzy and have a horrible head
Could look for some quinine. Got some during the day.

Crooke-Lawless came to see me. They took my temperature
And consulted over me, and told me I must go
To the hospital and cannot march with the battalion.

Went over to the farmhouse. There I found Matheson
Lying on a bed. He is pretty bad. I lay down
In the corner of the room. I have fever they tell me.

Sunday 4 March 1900

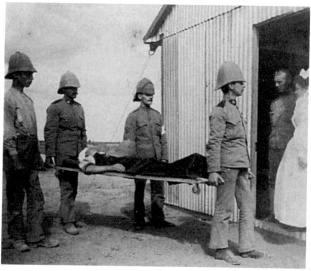

'A bad case, Sister'

Hors de Combat

I lay in the farmhouse till Tuesday
We have some condensed milk and some Liebig
In the morning we were got into wagons

The sun is very hot and they put some boughs
Over the wagon to keep it off
Just as were starting there was an alarm of Boers

Which delayed us for a bit and then we went on.
We all felt so seedy we did not care if there were Boers or not
We went to Jacobsdal and arrived there in the evening.

6 March 1900

Wynberg

Eventually arrived at Wynberg Hospital
Where I was sent to the Enteric Ward
Quite nice to lie down in a bed

Rather a depressing place this ward
One fellow awfully bad opposite me
In fact they are all pretty bad here.

11 12 13 March 1900

Progress of Sorts

They moved me from the Enteric Ward
The same day, as I am much better
And have turned bright yellow
Like a yellow Indian and have got jaundice.

Moved into the next ward where they have
Jaundice, dysentery and cases that are not wounds or enteric.
A civilian, Doctor Jamieson, who went to Bartholomew's Hospit.
Looks after me and seems to know his business

Wynberg Hospital

My ward in Wynberg Hospital is not a cheery place
As most of the inmates are feeling ill.
In the morning processions of people on stretchers
Are carried into the operating theatre

And return looking very flat.
In the afternoon there is generally a funeral passing.
I go for short walks but am rather shaky,
But I am rapidly getting better.

13-21 March 1900

Under Fire Again

I heard that a man among the cooks was supposed
To be able to cut hair etc.

We started early and marched to Six Mile Spruit
We had heard guns to our left front
During our march

I saw a newspaper correspondent and I asked
If there was any news of any sort.
He told me that Frankie Lloyd had been killed.

The two Coldstream Battalions then assembled
In quarter columns side by side, but below the skyline.
We were told to move to the right to make a right flank.

In the distance to our right, I saw some horsemen
And the naval guns put a shell close to them –
Then they scattered and made off.

I afterwards heard that they were some
Of our own mounted infantry, but I am not sure.
We got to the hill and beyond it was another

Where the enemy had taken up another position
About 1,500 yards away; the companies in the firing line
Lay down and fired away at them, and they fired back

A good many of the bullets dropping in our neighbourhood.
The bullets were falling at a pretty steep angle,
So fell amongst us though we were behind a slight rise.
One came just over me and got a man immediately
Behind me in the chest. We afterwards moved
A bit further to the right where we halted and firing

Went on till dusk. A lot of bullets kept landing about us
And knocking up dust. No. 7 Company was to my right
About 200 yards away and I went over to see them.

One man was in the act of taking a piece of paper,
Another man was handing to him, when a bullet came
And got him in the ankle. He had his pipe in his mouth,

But did not put it out and continued to smoke away
While he was tied up. They put him on a stretcher
And he was carried away still smoking and laughing.

4 June 1900

Surrender

All night long we heard trains
Shunting and whistling in Pretoria.

Standing to arms an hour before daylight
We made some little stone sangars

As best we could in the dark,
And wondered what sort of position

We should find ourselves in when the sun rose.
At daylight all was quiet.

We got our kettles from the rest
Of the battalion and had coffee,

And after waiting some time
We got a message to say that

'The town had surrendered –
But the men were not to cheer.'

And later we marched into the town.
We had a very dusty walk indeed of a mile or so

And halted near the railway station and then went on
For a little and halted in a pretty little street.

Tuesday 5 June 1900 Pretoria

Weapons Search

We were told we were to search the houses for arms
And various companies were told off to various blocks
Of houses. But I don't think it was very well organised,
As indeed there was not time. We began our search –
One went to a house and knocked –
If nobody came out we went in.

The houses were very nice, clean houses,
Pianos, nice beds, bathrooms etc. and in some
Breakfast was on the table, with a nice white table cloth;
And one was struck with the difference
Between all this, and our usual surroundings
And mode of life on the veldt.

I found a good many rifles; some were given up at once,
And then people said they had none.
If I found any after they had said they had none,
I sent the householder to the magistrate,
Who I believe was in an office somewhere with a report.
Most of the inhabitants were extremely civil,

But there were a few exceptions.
I had to do bit of house breaking
In some cases as the owners were away.
I was very sorry for one poor old lady
Who gave me her son's rifle in floods of tears
And said he had been killed fighting against the English.

5 June 1900 Pretoria

Diamond Hill

There was some burning grass
And I got a light for my pipe.

A regular storm of bullets
Came singing over our heads
But we were sheltered by the rocky ridge.
Some extraordinary accidents
However happened.

Butt, who I believe was sitting
Almost under a steep rock
Got a bullet through his leg,
And a few men were hit too
Though I can't think
Where the bullets came from.

Guards Brigade marching on Brandfort May1900

As we got to the top of the ridge
We got into some pretty sharp rifle fire.
One officer of Hamilton's Brigade near me
Said he thought the Boers
Were going to make a counter attack
And we could see movement of a some sort

Going on in the distance.
So I ran back to report to the C.O.
Who was with the battalion.
I don't think I ever ran so fast in my life
For the bullets came past me
And hit the ground round me as I ran.

I reported to the C.O. who sent
Some more companies up
And I took the remainder
Of my company and got back
To my other advanced sections.
They fired away till dark,
But we could not see much to fire at,
For the enemy did not show themselves.

And at dusk the grass on fire
About 500 yards in front of us blazed up,
Or at least one saw the red flame more
In the decreasing light, and from the sunset,
And with the darkness, firing ceased.

Tuesday 12 June 1900

Kraal near Diamond Hill

LONGUEVILLE POSTSCRIPT

When it came to the First War, Reginald Longueville was too old to serve and died peacefully near Oswestry in 1950 aged 81. His brother Edward and another younger brother called Francis Longueville did serve in the First War in the Coldstream Guards. Francis won the M.C. and the D.S.O. for conspicuous gallantry. Both survived the First War but sadly each of them had a son killed in the Second War: John Longueville killed at Salerno in 1943 and Reginald Francis Longueville killed in Holland in 1944. Both served in the Coldstream Guards.

Longueville Diaries

Gibraltar

Sir Robert Biddulph was an experienced army officer. He had served in the Crimean War and had been in the Indian Mutiny at the Relief of Lucknow. He served as assistant boundary commissioner for the Reform Act (1867) and was very much an army reformer working with Cardwell. He also served in Cyprus for a number of years and in 1893 became Governor of Gibraltar. In 1900 he oversaw a commission investigating alleged corruption with the purchase of 'remounts' for the army during the South African War.

The *Levanter* is the strong east wind that comes out of the Mediterranean and clips the Rock of Gibraltar.

Chlorodyne was invented by Dr Collis Browne a doctor in the Indian Army and consisted of laudanum, tincture of cannabis and chloroform. To be used for cholera, diarrhoea, insomnia, neuralgia and migraine. No doubt also useful if you got wounded or contracted enteric fever.

Geoffrey Fielding later became a Major General and was mentioned in despatches nine times, twice in the Boer War and seven times in the First War he also was awarded a D.S.O. and was knighted.

Life on the Ocean Wave

Colonel Codrington

Colonel Alfred Codrington was Commanding Office of the 1st Battalion Coldstream Guards. He was wounded twice in the Boer War and ended up as military secretary to Lord Kitchener in August 1914. He had seen much active service in Africa as well as Egypt in 1882, and was the son of General William Codrington who had been in the Crimean War. His grandfather was Admiral 'Navarino' Codrington. The sword he was sharpening may well have belonged to his father.

Captain Reginald Longueville was Officer Commanding No. 6 Company 1st Battalion Coldstream Guards. They sailed for South Africa leaving Gibraltar on 28 October

SS Malta *with 1st Coldstream Guards on board, approaching Cape Town in November 1899*

1899. The ship was the P&O liner *S.S. Malta*. They arrived in Cape Town on 16 November 1899 and within a week they were in action at the Battle of Belmont. Then in quick succession the battles of Graspan, Modder River and Magersfontien were followed by the assault on Cronjé's lair at Paarderberg.

Medical Matters

What is interesting is that they were even inoculated at all against enteric fever, otherwise known as typhoid. The vaccine had only just been discovered in 1896 by a British immunologist called Almroth Edward Wright who worked closely with the armed forces. How effective the inoculation was is open to debate as so many soldiers actually died from the disease. How many were inoculated before the war is not clear. Maybe the Guards Brigade coming out from England were lucky. After the Boer War, Almroth Wright managed to persuade the military authorities to vaccinate the whole army during the First World War and thus saved thousands of lives. Alexander Fleming followed in Wright's footsteps and when penicillin was discovered in 1928, Wright accurately predicted that its worldwide use would eventually lead to the creation of resistant strains of bacteria.

Major Crooke-Lawless ended up as Surgeon Lieut-Colonel Sir Warren Rowland Crooke-Lawless. He was born in Cork and served with the Coldstream Guards throughout the Boer War and was mentioned in despatches twice. He then served as surgeon to Lord Minto who was Viceroy to India. During the First World War Crooke-Lawless was mentioned in dispatches no less than six times and ended up as medical superintendent of Osborne House convalescent home for officers on the Isle of Wight.

The Briefing

After twenty days at sea without news it must have been very disconcerting to hear about one military mistake after another. Slowly the penny began to drop that the army had bitten off more than it could chew and that the Boer was a fine opponent who thought on his feet and was capable of unconventional military tactics.

Movement Orders

There was obviously, after the debacle in Natal and the bottling up of Ladysmith, Mafeking and Kimberley, an over riding desire to relieve at least one of the towns before Christmas and prove to the world that the British army was very competent. Easier said than done. Luckily for the British there was an efficient railway system to move troops around, but maps were very thin on the ground.

Touching Base

The distance from Cape Town to Orange River station was about five hundred miles. De Aar was the main military rail head where supplies and troops were initially gathered. It was also the base hospital where most of the wounded were later evacuated to. Being cooped up inside tents or corrugated iron huts must have been stifling in the summer months.

War Paint

Self explanatory. However officers were still fine targets as they were often taller then the men and were out in front. Not a good position to be in when Boer snipers are around. Despite the khaki, officer casualties were still very high indeed. In the Siege of Ladysmith some horses were even painted khaki.

Belmont 1 & 2

Lord Methuen was the general in charge. The maps were faulty and the plan ill conceived as the march took longer than expected and the kopjes had to be taken under bayonet in full daylight. The Boers, even though they were outnumbered four to one, had held a professional, highly disciplined and trained army of 8,000 men at bay for six to eight hours. Of the battle afterwards in his report Methuen stated 'I have accounted for 83 killed, and have 23 wounded in my hospital, and as their wounded were carried away I may assume their losses were heavier than mine'.

This is at variance with *The Natal Mercury* of 25 November which published a Reuter's dispatch from Belmont, giving the total British losses in Thursday's fight at 227, which number included 58 killed, 151 wounded, and 18 missing. Boer losses were officially

Welsh graves at Springfontein. All belong to senior medical staff at the Welsh Hospital who died of dysentery in June 1900. Dr Herbert Davies, Professor Thomas Jones and Nursing Sister Florence Louise Sage.

reported at 12 dead and 40 wounded, but the British buried at least 30 Boers found after the battle. It is estimated that the Boer losses were around one hundred. It was the first of many battles and the learning curve for Lord Methuen was not as steep as the kopjes.

The Grenadier officer mentioned, who was killed during the battle, was Lieutenant 'John' - Francis Lyall Fryer aged 26, son of Sir Francis Fryer of Rangoon, Burma.

Belts and Braces

This sounds a bit ominous, a bit like dead men's shoes, but there was an element of common sense about it. Officers even carried rifles and were often indistinguishable from the men they commanded.

Good Practice

This was after the Battle of Graspan, 25 November 1899. Sometimes it is called Enslin or Rooilaagte, names of villages nearby. A very similar battle to Belmont and just another station five miles up the line towards Kimberley. As with the Battle of Belmont, British casualties were about two hundred and the Boers retreated with minimal loss. The Boers also had ponies the British did not, so the 'P.B.I.' the 'Poor Bloody Infantry' had to slog it out in a route march under the heavy duty sun without water. No joke in the middle of a South African summer laden down with kit and a rifle. The lack of water, planning and forethought is appalling.

Modder River 1 - 4
28 November 1899

For details of this catastrophic
battle see previous notes. The
Coldstream Guards got off
relatively lightly in comparison
to the Argyll & Sutherland
Highlanders. The troops
walked straight into a trap
and the Boer trenches were
very well concealed. If the
Boers had held their fire till
the Coldstream Guards were
only five hundred yards away,

Ruggles Bryce

it would have been a real massacre. As it was the Boers
had indeed placed biscuit tins on the veld as range

Riet river

finders. They had
also painted white
stones on the railway
tracks. Buildings
were also obvious
targets. The mention
of the pom-pom is
interesting, an early
nickname for the
Maxim Nordenfelt heavy machine gun. Its bark was
sometimes worse than its bite. Lord Methuen and indeed
the Coldstream Guards had no idea that there was a
second river to cross called the Riet, a tributary of the
Modder.

After the Boers retreated the troops were given a day's
rest. Count Gleichen, as he was known was an officer in

the 3rd Grenadier Guards. He survived the Boer War and later became a Major General. He was Military Attaché to Berlin from 1903 to 1906 and fell out with Kaiser Wilhelm II. Gleichen also served in the First War and became Director of the Intelligence Bureau at the Department of Information from 1917 to 1918.

Winchester is a reference to Major Augustus John Paulet, 2nd Coldstream Guards otherwise known as The Marquess of Winchester. At 41 years old he was no spring chicken and was sadly killed a few days later at Magersfontein, taking reckless risks.

Rest and Recuperation

No rest for the wicked. As always it seems that orders are never really clear, and that both officers and men had to take whatever rest they could in between acting as guard picquets or fatigue parties. Modder River Camp fast became a kind of resort as it had once been for the citizens of Kimberley, though under very different circumstances.

Football match at Thebus camp

Magersfontein

The Guards Brigade were very lucky indeed not to suffer the fate of the Highland Division which was on their left flank. Colonel Codrington was wounded and the Marquess of Winchester was killed. In all the 1st Coldstreams lost thirteen men killed, with five officers and fifty men wounded. The 2nd Coldstreams had lost one officer and two men killed and twenty-two men wounded. A drop in the ocean compared with the losses in the Highland Brigade to their left.

About the casualties at Magersfontein, Conan Doyle had this to say: 'The most striking lesson of the engagement is the extreme bloodiness of modern warfare under some conditions, and its bloodlessness under others. Here, out of a total of something under a thousand casualties seven hundred were incurred in about five minutes, and the whole day of shell, machine-gun, and rifle fire only furnished the odd three hundred'.

Conan Doyle was full of praise for the medical officers. 'By ten o'clock on the morning after the battle, before the troops had returned to camp, no fewer than five hundred wounded were in the train and on their way back down the line to Cape Town.'

The next day the Coldstreams also got orders to retire, just as they had advanced at night, in quarter column. To Captain Reginald Longueville this 'seemed a very foolish thing to do as we were well within range of the enemy's guns'. Conan Doyle later commented that 'The Guards left the battle field as if on parade with the Boer shells bursting over their ranks.' Reginald Longueville notes in his diary in pencil that 'The Boers were only firing with one or two guns!'

Lucky Escape

As with so much in warfare patrolling is often the only way to gain accurate information. You either found nothing, got shot at, or if you very unlucky, wounded or even killed. The cavalry acting as mounted infantry were often thrown out on the flanks to probe defences and make observation. Their role became increasingly dangerous and were often leaving themselves open to ambush. Observation from balloons provided an overview but could not possibly pick out snipers or cleverly concealed trenches. The Royal Flying Corps and photographic reconnaissance became an important part of warfare in the First War for artillery spotting.

Snipers

This entry shows the extreme ranges of the Mauser and the Lee Metford, i.e. about one and a quarter miles. Lord Methuen was lucky that day. He was wounded and later captured by the Boers in March 1902.

Tarantula

Known as baboon spiders in South Africa, these large hairy spiders which can have a leg span of ten inches, always get bad press. Curiously the female tarantulas can live for as long as thirty years in the wild and the males only about ten years. They mate in the summer.

Scorpion

To be stung by a scorpion is not a pleasant experience. The centipede obviously knew what it was doing.

Chocolate

Queen Victoria obviously felt that her troops needed some supplement to their iron rations. It was a morale boost and they were designed as a New Year present for the troops for 1st January 1900. So the three major British chocolate manufacturers, Fry, Cadbury and Rowntree, all Quaker owned companies, produced the chocolate tins. Since 1854, Cadbury had a Royal Warrant to supply Queen Victoria with cocoa, so there was a question of conflicting loyalties at stake. These Quaker companies were against the war effort and were sticking to their pacifist principles, but they were eventually persuaded to fulfil their contracts.

The order was for 123,000 tins. In the end all three manufacturers refused to accept payment for the order and, not wishing to profit from the war, they offered to donate the chocolate instead. The manufacture of the tin boxes was funded personally by the Queen.

The troops could either eat the chocolate, make cocoa with it or send the tins back home to their loved ones. These red, blue and gold tins are now collector's items. The troops also found the tins very useful for collecting small mementos once the chocolate had been consumed.

Mahatma Gandhi notes wryly that civilians and unpaid volunteers, such as members of his Indian Bearer Corps, sometimes working under fire as stretcher bearers, were not considered eligible to receive the Queen's Chocolate. Maybe Gandhi was very fond of Chocolate!

Klip Drift

On 16 February 1900, the Coldstreams had repeated
their advance on Magersfontein and expecting to be fired
upon at any moment, eventually found that the trenches
were empty. The Boers had done a runner. The hunt was
on. The dead horses at Klip Drift belonged not only to the
Boers but to General French's cavalry who had ridden

Slightly wounded

through a few days earlier. Many horses had collapsed
after being ridden so hard. They were hot on the trail of
Cronjé who harboured up at Paardeberg, where he was
eventually run to ground. A bitter battle ensued which
developed into a siege of nearly ten days.

Last Supper

Often the Boers would kill their animals if they could not take them with them. The smell must have been particularly bad. It seems as though they had to leave in a hurry. They assumed that the British would simply follow the railway line all the way to Kimberley. General French had different ideas. With his force of 8,000 cavalry and 6,000 mounted infantry he overwhelmed a force of 900 Boers on a ridge at Klip Drift and caught them napping. It was amongst this scene of carnage that the Coldstream Guards had to camp. Holding Klip Drift was vital.

Médecins Sans Frontières

Doctors like war correspondents sometimes had a remarkable degree of freedom. In the Boer War there were Russian ambulances and French ambulances as well as Dutch ambulances and American ambulances. All horse drawn of course. They tagged on the end of the particular national commandos. Soldiers were always aware that the bush had eyes and ears, and that spies were often passing information about their movements and troop dispositions. It seems that this doctor was taking a great risk trying to get through siege lines to Cronjé. A brave thing to do.

The sound of gunfire in the east was the closing stages of the Battle of Paardeberg which means 'Horse Mountain' or perhaps in this case more appropriately 'Dead Horse Gulch'.

En Passage

When Cronjé surrendered over four thousand Boers were captured and much of their equipment destroyed. It had been a costly battle on both sides. The British lost 348 killed and nearly 1,000 wounded. A decisive victory had been won, but it was only the beginning. About fifty Boer women were inside the camp and some were in the front line firing. At least two were found dead. Cronjé's wife was also captured and later accompanied her husband when he was sent to St Helena.

Major Albrecht bound for St Helena with his chums, captured at Paardeberg, including Major Baron Von Dewitz, the famous German military engineer.

Such was the intensity of battle inside Cronjé's laager that a sentry found asleep and woken by General Ferreira, shot the general by mistake. Major Albrecht eventually ran out of ammunition and was thus out of a job. He was an ex-Prussian artilleryman and veteran of the 1870-1871 War, and had served in the 4th Prussian Guard Artillery Regiment.

Chief Commandant M. J. Wolmarans, Kruger's brother-in-law, was also sent to St Helena. So Reginald Longueville was meeting some very interesting people, and even photographing the Boer prisoners as they passed by. History in the making.

Piet Cronjé under escort with umbrella. Klip Drift 28 Feb 1900

Fever

Luckily for Reginald Longueville it was only jaundice and not enteric fever that he had. It may well be that the inoculation worked for him or else it was the Chlorodyne. It also sounds as if he may have had tick typhus as well. Not a good combination.

Hors de Combat

Reginald Longueville was very lucky to get hold of both condensed milk and 'Liebig' meat extract. Liebig was in fact a molasses-like black spread usually sold in an opaque white glass bottle, and contained only reduced meat stock and salt (4%). It takes 3 kg of meat to make 100 g of extract and was invented by Justus Von Liebig. Oxo was a cheaper version

introduced in 1899. Justus Liebig is also considered by some the 'father of the fertilizer industry' for his discovery of nitrogen as an essential plant nutrient. His work was later continued by Fritz Haber who invented the Haber process and we have had artificial fertiliser ever since.

Wynberg

This is No. 1 General Hospital Wynberg on the outskirts of Cape Town and one of the main hospitals. If patients were very ill or needed prolonged convalescence they were often sent back to England.

Progress of Sorts

By mid April, Reginald Longueville was fit for army duties again and is sent to Springfontein via De Aar. He then takes part in the actions around Vet River, Zand River, Brandfort and Bloemfontein.

Under Fire Again

This action took place near Six Mile Spruit on the advance to Pretoria. Lieutenant Colonel Francis Lloyd was commanding the 2nd Grenadier Guards. In fact Lieut-Col Lloyd was not killed but he was severely wounded in May 1900 at Biddulphsberg in the Orange Free State. This is where the 2nd Grenadier Guards were caught between a wild bush fire and the fire of the Boers. No one knows who set the tall grass alight behind the British lines. The casualties were very high and over one hundred wounded men later died of burns sustained in the fire. Colonel Lloyd survived and went on to become a Lieut-General and was responsible for the defence of

London against Zeppelin attacks in the First World War. Fire of a different sort.

Amazingly the man hit in the chest survived. He was called Howarth and later became a policeman in Oxford and rose to the rank of inspector.

Changing helmets for hats

Surrender

Many people, politicians, generals even war correspondents thought that once Pretoria surrendered the war would be over. How wrong they were. The guerrilla war went on for another two years. The noise of trains was the Kruger Government doing a runner. Kruger himself ended up in Holland and eventually died in Switzerland. To this day some people wonder where the Kruger millions are buried.

Weapons Search

A common enough and necessary action but no doubt an unpleasant one in certain circumstances. Weapons were often piled up and burnt.

Diamond Hill

The war did not stop just because Pretoria had surrendered. This battle was decisive and the British troops who numbered about 14,000 drove some 4,000 Boers off a hill to the east of Pretoria. After that the system of warfare changed radically and it became far more of a guerrilla war.

The Coldstream Guards were then based at Waterval Onder and in Cape Colony at Thebus. The war became an increasingly bitter game of cat and mouse with no end in sight.

The Coldstream Guards at Diamond Hill

Part 8

The Lost Cause

This extract is from the last chapter of *Commando* by **Deneys Reitz** and brilliantly describes the conflicting emotions on the Boer side as they draw near to the end of the war in late April 1902. It also shows the enormous degree of respect shown to the commando leaders by all ranks of the British army as they travel to Vereeniging to chew over the peace terms offered by Kitchener.

Freedom

On the surface things looked prosperous.
Five months ago
we had come into this western country
hunted like outlaws, and to-day
we practically held the whole area
from the Olifants to the Orange River
four hundred miles away.

Save for small garrison towns here and there,
whose occupants could not show themselves
beyond the range of their forts
without the risk of instant capture
at the hands of the rebel patrols told off to watch them,
while we roamed all the territory at will.

We had enjoyed a number of successes
which the British probably regarded as minor incidents,
but which our men looked upon as important victories
and all this had greatly raised their spirits.

Unfortunately, while matters stood thus well with us,
the situation in the two Republics up north
was far otherwise. Lord Kitchener's relentless policy
of attrition was slowly breaking the hearts of the commandos.

We had been out of touch with them for so long
that we did not realize the desperate straits
to which they had come, and our men judged the position
from our own more favourable circumstances.

Personally, I was not quite so sanguine,
for, from such English newspapers as had come my way,
I had learned something of the true state of affairs,
but I hoped that all would yet be well
and I kept my thoughts to myself.

The White Flag

Towards the end of April I rode out one afternoon
with Duncker and Nicolas Swart
to snipe at the English posts on the other side of O'Okiep,
and, as we were returning to our horses,
we saw a cart coming along the road from the south
with a white flag waving over the hood.

Galloping up, we found two British officers inside
who said that they were the bearers
of a dispatch from Lord Kitchener.
We took them to Concordia,
our pickets amongst the hills riding down

from all sides to hear what it was about,
but the officers professed ignorance
of the contents of their message,
although I had an uneasy suspicion of the truth.

When we reached Concordia,
General Smuts took them inside his house
and remained closeted with them for some time,
after which he came out and walked away
into the veld by himself in deep thought.

We knew then that there was grave news.

Safe Conduct

That evening he showed me the dispatch.
It was a communication from Lord Kitchener
to say that a meeting - between the English and Boer leaders
was to be held at Vereeniging,
on the banks of the Vaal River,
with a view to discussing peace terms,
and he was summoned to attend.

A safe-conduct pass was enclosed,
under which he was to proceed
through the English lines to Port Nolloth,
where he would be taken by sea to Cape Town,
and from there by rail to the Transvaal.

All this was ominous,
and he spoke forebodingly of the future,
but, in spite of the shadow that hung over us,
one item almost made me forget the darker side,
for the safe-conduct provided
for a Secretary and an Orderly,
and he said that I was to go with him as one of these.

I was so delighted at the prospect of going on a journey
like this that for the time being I gave thought to little else.

The men were the real tragedy.
They had endured against great odds,
facing years of peril and hardship without pay or reward,
and they still had so much faith in the cause
for which they were fighting that,
when the news trickled through next day
that General Smuts was to go to a peace conference,
they were convinced that the British were suing
for terms and were ready to restore our country.

It was pitiful to listen to their talk,
and to see their faces light up
when they spoke of having won through at last,
and I, for one, had not the heart to disillusion them,
or even to hint at a result other than favourable,
so steadfast was their trust.

Jan Smuts and Charlie

Farewell

General Smuts set to work at once.
Next morning a messenger was sent into O'Okiep,
to advise the garrison that both sides were to refrain
from active military operations while the Congress lasted,
and the two British officers went on ahead
to Steinkopf, to warn the relief force collecting there
that we were shortly passing through their-pickets.

The day after that the commando came in
from the out-lying posts to say good-bye to their leader.
The men paraded before the Court House,
each man sitting his horse, rifle at thigh,
while General Smuts addressed them.

He briefly told them of the object of his going,
and asked them to be prepared for disappointment
if need be, but there were only cheers and shouts of courage,
as they pressed from all sides to wish him farewell.

I steered through the throng to shake hands
with such as I could reach, waving to others beyond,
and in this way I saw the last
of many good friends and companions.

Orderly Business

We set off next day, escorted by a small patrol.
I left my spare horses, rifle, and gear
with Nicolas Swart and Edgar Duncker,
my best friends, whom I have not met again.
We reached van Deventer's commando
that afternoon where they were watching the troops
that had come up from the sea,
and for the last time we spent a night around camp fires.
In the morning we made ready to pass
into the English lines.

As we started, General Smuts told me
that his brother in law, Krige,
was the other man to accompany him,
and he said we were to arrange amongst ourselves
which was to be Secretary and which Orderly,
so I chose to be Orderly,

as I thought it meant an aide-de-camp,
and left my companion to be Secretary.

Soon after that we saddled our horses,
said good-bye to van Deventer and his men,
and rode down the valley towards the English lines.
Far down we were met by Colonel Collins,
who commanded the relief expedition.

Here our escort took over our horses,
and, after singing our Commando Hymn,
and firing a farewell volley into the air,
they wheeled round and galloped cheering away
towards their own side,
to the manifest interest of the English officers
and troopers lined up beside the road.
With them went the last of our free life
and all that it had meant to us.
A cart was brought, in which General Smuts,
Krige, and I were driven to a large camp
standing beside the railway line,
where a guard of honour was drawn up to receive us,
behind which crowds of soldiers had gathered
to see the Boer Emissaries.

I now discovered that I had made a mistake,
and that an Orderly was an officer's batman,
whereas a Secretaryship carried commissioned rank.

Krige was invited into Colonel Collins's tent
with General Smuts, while I was led to the servants' mess,
and when, an hour later, a train stood ready to take us
to Port Nolloth he and General Smuts
were ceremoniously ushered into a first-class compartment,
whilst I was put aboard an open cattle-truck with the luggage.

However, being in an enemy camp
and travelling by rail for the first time
for nearly two years was so exciting
that it made no difference to me where I was,
and Krige and I appreciated the humorous side
of our respective positions.

Whenever he looked out of the carriage window
and saw me sitting in the truck behind,
he roared with laughter, and so did I,
at his having become an officer, and I a servant.

When the train drew up at the next station
there was another guard of honour
for General Smuts and his Secretary,
who were taken in to a grand luncheon,
whilst I foregathered with the batmen
in the kitchen behind.

At the next halting-place
I underwent record promotion.

There was an officer of the Hussars, Captain Barclay,
who had been deputed to accompany us to the coast,
and having seen me standing about,
he asked General Smuts who I was.

The General explained that on commando
there were no social distinctions,
but that he had brought me along
because he thought my father might be at the Conference.

Captain Barclay telephoned up the line to Colonel Collins,
to say that a son of the Transvaal State Secretary
was of the party as an orderly,
and he presently came to me and said,
'Young man, you are Chief-of-Staff to General Smuts;
come along and join us.'

He jokingly assured me that the promotion
from batman to field rank
in the course of one morning
was the quickest known in any army.

Sea Voyage

Towards evening we reached Port Nolloth,
a dreary little seaport,
where many troopships lay at anchor.
One of these, the *Lake Erie*, was under steam,
and even as the train ran into the station,
a boat set out to fetch us.

Port Nolloth

This was the end of our long roving.
We stood on the quayside,
silently looking back on the way we had come,
each busy with his own thoughts.

I do not know what was in the minds
of my companions, but perhaps they, too,
were thinking of the long road we had travelled,
of camp-fires on mountains and plains,
and of the good men and splendid horses that were dead.

With heavy hearts we got into the boat
that was to take us to the ship,
and the moment we were on board they weighed anchor,
and we sailed southward.

In spite of our mission,
the voyage was one of great pleasure to me.
After years of rough fare and hard living,
we had luxurious cabins, with soft beds to lie on;
a steward with coffee in the morning,
a bath ready prepared and food
such as I had almost forgotten the existence of.
All this seemed like a dream, and I enjoyed every moment of it.

We reached Capetown in five days,
and were trans-shipped to Simonstown
on board the battleship *Monarch*, with Captain Parkes,
and here again we spent a week in comfort,
for officers and men vied with each other
in their efforts to welcome us.

The British, with all their faults,
are a generous nation, and not only on the man-of-war,
but throughout the time that we were amongst them,
there was no word said that could hurt our feelings
or offend our pride, although they knew
that we were on an errand of defeat.

Meeting Lord Kitchener

At length orders came for us to go north.

We were rowed ashore after dark
to a landing-stage below the Simonstown railway station,
and taken to a train that was standing ready.
We were hurried through the suburbs of Capetown
and then switched on to the main line at Salt River Junction,
to find ourselves at Matjesfontein in the Karroo next day.

Here General French came to see us,
a squat, ill-tempered man, whom we did not like,
although he tried to be friendly.
He sat talking to us for an hour or more
trying to draw General Smuts,
who had no difficulty in parrying his clumsy questions.
When he made no head-way,
he became more natural and spoke of his experiences –
during the war, in the course of which
he told us how narrowly
we had missed capturing him that night
below the Stormbergen.

From Matjesfontein we continued our journey,
travelling at night only, an armoured train
puffing ahead all the way, its searchlight sweeping the veld.
Each day we were side-tracked
at some lonely spot till dark,
and thus made slow progress.

I have been told that we were purposely delayed lest,
coming from the Cape where the outlook was brighter,
we might persuade the Transvaalers
that things were not so bad as they seemed.
For this reason Lord Kitchener
did not wish us to appear amongst them
until matters had gone too far for them to turn back.

However that may be, it took us
the better part of a week
to reach Kroonstad in the Northern Free State,
where Lord Kitchener was to meet us.
Soon after our arrival he rode up to the station
on a magnificent black charger,
followed by a numerous suite,
including turbaned Pathans,
in Eastern costume with gold-mounted scimitars.

His retinue waited outside
while he came into our compartment to talk.
He was anxious to bring the war to a close,
for he referred again and again
to the hopelessness of our struggle,
telling us that he had four hundred thousand troops
in South Africa against our eighteen thousand.

He said that he was prepared
to let the burghers retain their horses and saddles
in recognition of the fight that they had made,
and that the British Government would help
to rebuild the destroyed farmhouses,
the burning of which he defended on military grounds.

General Smuts taxed him
with having unfairly executed our men in the Cape,
and this, too, he justified, on the plea
that we had used khaki uniforms to decoy his soldiers.

Before going he told us that we were to proceed
to the Eastern Transvaal, to find General Botha,
and that the conference at Vereeniging
would only take place after that.

Botha and Biltong

Accordingly, from Kroonstad,
still escorted by an armoured train,
we crossed the Vaal River into the Transvaal.

Louis Botha

We went through Johannesburg at night,
and here they turned us east on to the Natal line,
until we came to the town of Standerton,
where we left the train and travelled by cart
along a block-house line
that ran straight over the high veld.

At intervals there were small English camps,
at each of which the troops turned out
and treated us with courtesy.

We journeyed for a day and-a half,
until we reached a point where a party of horsemen
sent by General Botha was awaiting us.
They had brought spare horses,
so we left the cart with the troopers,
and, striking across country,
travelled for two days over bare and deserted plains,
to the place where the Commandant-General
was expecting us.
Here about three hundred men were assembled.
They were delegates from every commando
in the Eastern Transvaal,
come to elect representatives to the Peace Congress
to be held at Vereeniging,
and nothing could have proved more clearly
how nearly the Boer cause was spent
than these starving, ragged men,
clad in skins or sacking, their bodies covered with sores,

from lack of salt and food,
and their appearance was a great shock to us,
who came from the better-conditioned forces in the Cape.

Their spirit was daunted,
but they had reached the limit of physical endurance,
and we realised that, if these haggard, emaciated men
were the pick of the Transvaal commandos,
then the war must be irretrievably lost.

Koos de la Rey

Christiaan de Wet

Food was so scarce that General Botha himself
had only a five strips of leathery biltong to offer us,
and he said that, but for the lucky chance
of having raided a small herd of cattle
from the British a fortnight before,
he would have been unable to hold the meeting at all.

I inquired at once for news
of my father and my three brothers.
General Botha gave me word of my father.

He told me that he was with one of the northern commandos,
and would in all probability be at the coming Conference.
He could tell me nothing of my brothers,
but by asking among the men,
I learned that my eldest brother, Hjalmar,
had been captured by the Australians
more than a year before,
and that my second brother, Joubert,
was taken prisoner whilst lying ill
of malarial fever in the low country,
apparently not long after I had last seen him
at the Warm Baths, towards the end of 1900.
I could find out nothing about my youngest brother Arnt.

My Father

Next day the elections were held.
Even in adversity the Boer instinct for speeches
and wordy wrangling asserted itself,
and the time was passed in oratory,
and with nominations and re-nominations of candidates,
but by evening the complicated balloting was finished,
and some thirty delegates elected.

Next morning the gathering dispersed,
the men riding off on their hungry-looking horses
to rejoin their distant units,
while General Botha and the successful deputies
started back for the English block-house line.

We arrived here by the following evening.
The troops supplied us with food,
for we were famishing,
and we now returned along the block-houses to Standerton,
the soldiers everywhere standing respectfully
to attention as our tattered cavalcade went by.

At Standerton we entrained for Vereeniging.
This is a small mining village on the banks of the Vaal River,
where, nearly two years before,
I had watched the Irishmen burning the railway stores
during the retreat from the south.

The British had prepared a large tented camp
for our reception, and almost the first man I saw
as we entered was my father, shaggy and unkempt,
but strong and well, and our greeting
after so long a parting was deep and heartfelt.

And now the delegates came in from the rest of the Transvaal
and from the Free State. Every leader of note was there.

General de la Rey, Christiaan de Wet,
President Steyn, Beyers, Kemp, and many others,
the best of the Boer fighting-men.

We learned from General de Wet
that my younger brother had been serving under him

Warrior farmers – Commandant de Wet and his sons

for more than a year,
and that he was still safe and sound,
so we were all accounted for.
Although two were prisoners of war,
we had been luckier than the majority of families,
most of whom were mourning their dead,
whereas all five of us were still alive.

Exile

I know little of the actual Peace Conference
as I was not a delegate, but the outcome
was a foregone conclusion.
Every representative had the same disastrous tale
to tell of starvation, lack of ammunition, horses,
and clothing, and of how the great block-house system
was strangling their efforts to carry on the war.

Added to this was the heavy death-roll
among the women and children,
of whom twenty-five thousand had already died
in the concentration camps,
and the universal ruin that had overtaken the country.

Every homestead was burned,
all crops and live-stock destroyed,
and there was nothing left but to bow to the inevitable.

After prolonged debates the Conference
suspended its sittings for a day, whilst General Botha,
my father, General de la Rey and others went to Pretoria
to conclude the final treaty with Lord Kitchener and Lord Milner.
On their return peace was an accomplished fact.

Of the sting of defeat – I shall not speak,
but there was no whining or irresponsible talk.
All present accepted the verdict stoically,
and the delegates returned quietly to their respective commandos,
to make known the terms of surrender.

I was spared the ordeal of returning
to break the news to our men in the Cape,
for my father insisted upon my remaining with him
when General Smuts went south.

When he came to take leave of me,
he said that he dreaded the task of telling the men,
and our hearts were heavy at the thought
of the disappointment awaiting them.

We shook hands for the last time, and then he, too, was gone.

My father was sent into the low country,
to arrange for the bringing in of the commando
with which he had been serving.

We travelled by rail to Balmoral Station on the Delagoa Bay line,
and from there on horseback into the wild country
through which my brother and I had ridden
in search of General Beyers, earlier in the war.

After two days hard going we found the camp,
and my father had the unpleasant duty of telling the men
that all was over. Most of them took it calmly,
but some cursed and vowed hat they would never surrender.

My father, although he had himself voted against peace
at the Conference, pointed out to them that they should
either submit to what had been done,
or leave the country, as he intended doing.

This quieted the more turbulent,
and we started back next day for Balmoral,
where the men were to hand in their rifles.

This depressing ceremony was presided over
by an English officer, seated at a table beneath the trees,
with a regiment of troops in reserve close by.

Despite his protests, our men fired away
their ammunition into the air,
smashed their rifle-butts and sullenly flung
the broken weapons down,
before putting their names to the undertaking
which each man was called upon to sign,
that he would abide by the peace terms.

When my father's turn came,
he handed over his rifle to the officer in charge,
but refused to sign.

He said that although he was one of the signatories
to the Peace Treaty, he had told Lord Milner
at the time that he was setting his hand to the document
in his official capacity as State Secretary of the Transvaal
and not as a private individual,
and Lord Milner had accepted his signature on that basis.

The officer pointed out that he would not be allowed
to remain in the country, and my father agreed.
I had no very strong convictions on the subject,
but I had to stand by him,
so I also refused to sign,
and was told that I would be put across the border,
which troubled me little,
as I was eager to see more of the world.

When all was over, the men rode off
on their different ways, to search
for what remained of their families and ruined homes.

My father and I went to Balmoral Station,
where a message had been received from Lord Milner
confirming the order that we were to be deported,
but qualifying it to the extent of allowing
my father a fortnight in which to settle his affairs in Pretoria.

And so we returned, after more than two years of wandering.

We found our home in the possession
of a British General with sentries outside
who forbade approach.
Our household goods had disappeared,
and had it not been for the hospitality of a friend
we should have gone roofless.

During this time my younger brother
came riding in from the Free State,
six inches taller than when I last saw him,
and none the worse for his long adventure.

He, too, decided to go, and so, towards the end of June,
we went into self-imposed exile.

As we were waiting on the border at Komati Poort,
before passing into Portuguese territory,
my father wrote on a piece of paper a verse which he gave me.

It ran:

SOUTH AFRICA

Whatever foreign shores my feet must tread,
My hopes for thee are not yet dead.
Thy freedom's sun may for a while be set,
– But not for ever, God does not forget.

And he said that until liberty came
to his country he would not return.

He is now in America and my brother and I
are under the French flag in Madagascar.
We have heard of my other two brothers.
The eldest has reached Holland
from his Prison camp in India,
and the other is still in Bermuda awaiting release.

Maritz and Robert de Kersauson
are with us in Madagascar.
We have been on an expedition far down
into the Sakalave country,
to see whether we could settle there.

General Gallieni provided us with riding-mules
and a contingent of Senegalese soldiers,
as those parts are still in a state of unrest.

It was like going to war again,
but all went quietly, and we saw much
that was of interest - lakes and forests;
swamps teeming with crocodiles,
and great open plains grazed by herds of wild cattle.
But for all its beauty the island repels one
in some intangible manner, and in the end we shall not stay.

At present we are eking out a living
convoying goods by ox-transport between
Mahatsara on the East Coast and Antananarive,
hard work in dank fever-stricken forests,
and across mountains sodden with eternal rain;
and in my spare time I have written this book.

Antananarive Madagascar 1903

 Note: William Reitz's father - FW - Francis William Reitz, as Secretary of State of the Transvaal Republic, had attended the ill fated Bloemfontein Peace conference back in June 1899 with Paul Kruger. Both of them had to spar with Sir Alfred Milner. A lot of water and lives had passed under the railway bridge since those days.

In the First World War Deneys Reitz helped suppress the Maritz Rebellion and then served under Jan Smuts when fighting in German West Africa and in German East Africa. He later served in the British army where he commanded the First Battalion Royal Scots Fusiliers and was severely wounded in early 1918.

Commando was written in Madagascar but not published until 1929.

Deneys Reitz in Namaqualand with Jan Smuts

Are there any Boers about?
De-bagged. Long John to the rescue.

Bibliography

AMERY, LEOPOLD S. *Times History of the War in South Africa.* 7 vols. 1899-1902

ANON. *Khaki in South Africa. An Album of Pictures and Photographs illustrating the chief events of the War under Lord Roberts.*1900

BREYTENBACH, J.H. *Die Geskiedenis van die Tweede Vryheidsoorlog in Suid-Afrika, 1899-1902.* 6 vols. 1969-96

BROWN, HAROLD & GREW, E. SHARPE. *War with the Boers. An Account of the Past and Present Troubles with the South African Republics.* 5 vols.1900-02

BURLEIGH, BENNET. *The Natal Campaign.* 1900

BURNETT, Major CHARLES. *The 18th Hussars in South Africa.* 1905

CLEAVER, REGGIE MOSTYN & FENTON, MARGUERITE DE. *The War Letters of an English Burgher.* With an Introduction by Simon Gray. 2000. First published in 1913 as *A Young South African*

CRESWICKE, LOUIS. *South Africa and the Transvaal War.* 8 vols.1900-03

DAVIS, RICHARD HARDING. *With Both Armies.* 1900

DAVIS, RICHARD HARDING. *Notes from a War Correspondent.* 1912

DAVITT, MICHAEL. *The Boer Fight for Freedom.*1902

DOYLE, Sir ARTHUR CONAN. *The Great Boer War.* 1901

HEYNINGEN, ELIZABETH VAN. *The Concentration Camps of the Anglo-Boer War.* 2013

HUNTER, ARCHIE. *Kitchener's Sword-Arm: The Life and Campaigns of Sir Archibald Hunter.* 1996

JUTA, MARJORIE. *The Pace of the Ox.* The Life of Paul Kruger. 1937

LYNCH, GEORGE. *Impressions of a War Correspondent.* 1902

MACDONALD, WILLIAM T*he Romance of the Golden Rand* 1933

PAKENHAM, THOMAS *The Boer War* 1979

PRETORIUS, FRANSJOHAN *The Anglo-Boer War* 1988

RALPH, JULIAN *Towards Pretoria. A Record of the War between Briton and Boer to the Hoisting of the British Flag at Bloemfontein* 1900

REITZ, DENEYS *Commando. A Boer Journal of the Boer War* 1929

SMITH, M. VAN WYK *Drummer Hodge: The Poetry of the Anglo-Boer War.* 1978

STEEVENS, G.W. *From Capetown to Ladysmith.* 1900

WET, CHRISTIAAN RUDOLF DE. *Three Years War.* 1902

WILSON, LADY SARAH. *South African Memories: Social, Warlike & Sporting.* 1909

WILSON, H.W. *With the Flag to Pretoria.* 2 vols. 1900

WILSON, H.W. *After Pretoria: The Guerrilla War.* 2 vols. 1902

'Single to Cape Town please.'

Photographic Credits

The Boer war was one of the first wars to be covered by both journalists and photographers. Sadly there are very few real action shots as the Boer marksmen would have spotted a photographer with his tripod and camera, a mile off. And that would have been curtains. Also the shutter speed was critical, but they were more often than not blessed with strong clear light. For the last two years much of the war was a guerrilla war with hit and run raids at night, so the opportunities for photography were limited. Having said all that, there are very wide range of photographs of places and people on both sides. Stereo views were all the rage and an American Firm, Underwood and Underwood specialised in these.

Some officers used The No 2 Folding Kodak Pocket Camera model A with leather bellows which could be slipped into the pocket. It cost £2/10 shillings. The first Brownie box camera was introduced in February 1900 and the box was made of cardboard. It took 2¼ inch square pictures and cost 5/-. Even some of the Boer

prisoners of war were able to get hold of them and used them in their prison camps in Ceylon.

Contemporary magazines and books are laden with photographs of the war and personalities and are a rich resource in their own right. The early set piece battles are not very well covered and many illustrations have relied upon sketches both real and imaginary. It was the cross over point between real war photography and dramatic heroic oil paintings, much beloved by the Victorians.

On the Boer side there were also many very good photographers, some attracted by the gold fields and diamond mining. They would have had access to all the studio and laboratory facilities at the beginning of the war, at least till Bloemfontein, Johannesburg and Pretoria were captured.

Most photographs and illustrations have been gleaned from contemporary books and articles c 1900. In most cases the photographers are unknown, but I have managed to track down two army officers who took some excellent pictures which have never been published before. These credits are given below:

Captain Reginald Longueville, 1st Coldstream Guards. His photographs appear on pages: 30, 44, 47, 52-3, 78, 97, 102, 135, 160, 182, 196-7, 211, 222, 249, 290-1, 292, 294, 295, 302, 304, 310, 313, 314, 316, 318, 319, 322, 322-5, 326 ,330-1, 334, 336, 343, 337, 350, 351, 352, 353, 360, 362, 400 by kind permission of Anthony Norton.

All Longueville's photographs © Anthony Norton

Photographs taken by Captain Edward, Simpson South African Light Horse © James Payne 'Through Their Eyes' **www.throughtheireyes2.co.uk**
21, 99, 102, 103, 121, 228, 230, 314, 399. Other photos of SALH: 11, 12, 111, 139, 204, 205, 214, 219, 237, 257, 270, 289, 301 © James Payne

Photo page 64 of Lt Percy Evans-Freke © Leicestershire Yeomanry and by kind permission of Robert Boyle.

Postscript

Interestingly the First the German Navy Law enabling Germany to start a massive shipbuilding programme was passed in 1898, only two years after the Jameson Raid. The Second Navy Law which doubled the size of their fleet was passed in June 1900 after three German mail ships were stopped off the African coast and searched by British cruisers looking for materiel and weapons which might be on their way help the Boers. There were three more Navy Laws in 1906, 1908, and 1912 by which time the Kaiser was feeling very pleased with himself. He had caught Granny's Navy up at last. All he needed was a match to light the fuse.

So in a sense the Jameson Raid and the Boer War indirectly kick started the arms race which led directly to the debacle of 1914.

mailme @ james - crowden
www.james-crowden.co.uk